"At the heart of all they do, David and Lis[...] families and healthy relationships. Their [...] stand, and filled with helpful, real-life exa[...] write as they teach—with love, compassion, and challenges [...] directions."

—Linda A. Miner, PhD
Professor
Southern Nazarene University—Tulsa

"David and Lisa Frisbie are truly gifted authors of many excellent books with a wealth of experience. They help individuals and couples enrich their lives through godly principles and many examples of real life in action. I would highly recommend adding them to your list of must-read authors."

—Pastor Gary Vanderford
North Coast Church
Vista, California

"Dave and Lisa Frisbie are consistently a godly, wise, prayerful, compassionate, and truthful voice in the midst of ministry joys and chaos. There is no better friend to those in ministry than the Frisbies!"

—Rev. Bob and Linda Reter

"I have appreciated the work of Dr. David and Lisa Frisbie. I am sure you will find their new writing, *Managing Stress in Ministry,* to be very informative and helpful. By applying the principles in this writing, you will not only extend your ministry effectiveness but also find deep fulfillment personally."

—Dr. Daniel R. Gales
Author, *The Complete Spiritual Gifts Kit*

"As a physician involved in a busy medical practice, I have found Dr. David and Lisa Frisbie's insight a wonderful, practical tool in balancing the stress of life in healthy ways."

—Michael J. Martin, MD
Tulsa, Oklahoma

"*Managing Stress in Ministry* is a *must* for anyone in a serving vocation! The Frisbies bring their vast reservoir of knowledge and experience to help those in ministry avoid and cope with burnout and stress."

—Anne A. Ghost Bear, EdD
Director
Southern Nazarene University—Tulsa

"Over the years, I have observed David and Lisa follow God's leading, which has immersed them in the demands of ministry. Despite the stresses, they remain a steady and strong team as they seek to bring healing and wholeness to lives impacted by a broken world."

—Tim Keeton
Associate Vice President for University Advancement
MidAmerica Nazarene University

"*Managing Stress in Ministry* is a timely road map for Christian workers who yearn to deal with life's challenges in a productive and healthy way. Though levels of stress increase and decrease during the chapters of our life, none of us are immune to the reality of stress. Poorly managed stress can damage or weaken our health, our marriage, our family, and our ministry. We are indebted to David and Lisa Frisbie for skillfully giving us practical tools for Christ-glorifying stress management."

—Dr. Jerry D. Porter
General Superintendent
Church of the Nazarene

"David and Lisa Frisbie understand anyone in ministry today is dealing with multiple, equal priorities vying for one's attention. Handling that stress with peace and confidence is what we all long for. They get it!"

—Carol Best
Public Relations Manager
MidAmerica Nazarene University

"David and Lisa Frisbie's preaching, teaching, and public and private counseling ministries over the last twenty-seven years of our friendship have been extraordinarily extensive and compassionate."

—Rodger and Sharon Manning

"If you have come to realize that life is stress and you need to learn how to deal with it, David and Lisa Frisbie's fresh insights into life's relentless strains provide helpful strategies for finding peace in the midst of the storms."

—Woodie J. Stevens
Global SDMI Director
Church of the Nazarene

MANAGING
STRESS
IN MINISTRY

MANAGING STRESS IN MINISTRY

DAVID & LISA FRISBIE

BEACON HILL PRESS
OF KANSAS CITY

Copyright 2014 by David Frisbie and Lisa Frisbie

ISBN 978-0-8341-3220-7

Printed in the
United States of America

Cover Design: Matt Johnson
Interior Design: Sharon Page

All Scripture quotations not otherwise designated are from *The Holy Bible, New International Version®* (NIV®). Copyright © 1973, 1978, 1984, 2011 by Biblica, Inc.™ Used by permission of Zondervan. All rights reserved worldwide.

Permission to quote from the following copyrighted version of the Bible is acknowledged with appreciation:

New King James Version (NKJV). Copyright © 1979, 1980, 1982 by Thomas Nelson, Inc.

10 9 8 7 6 5 4 3 2 1

DEDICATION

This book is for pastors and their families, written as a labor of love.

We love pastors, their marriage partners, and their children. We love serving them in any way we can. From speaking at PK events to counseling and helping at Ministers and Mates Retreats, in a wide range of ways, God allows us to serve and help pastors and their families. We love serving and helping.

For the people in the parsonage—men and women, teens and children—we have only respect and love. Some of the best and brightest people we know serve in pastoral ministry, in places that are rural or urban, in congregations that are large or small. There is no correlation between the size of the church and the importance of the pastor. We know amazingly wise, deeply mature Christian leaders who are faithfully tending their flocks in small places, far away from news media, headlines, fame, and fortune.

These men and women serve because God called them, not because they seek power or importance, money or possessions. They serve from a strong sense of divine imperative; ministry is what God has asked them to do.

Their heart's desire is to say a resounding "Yes!" to God's call. They are responding to him and to his design for their lives. God sees their service and honors their labor with his harvest, in his time and his way.

Since this book is *for* pastors and their families, it seems only natural that we would dedicate this book *to* pastors and their families. We will begin with "families" and work our way around to some of the most amazing pastors we've met along the contours of our journey.

Here are some of the people to whom this new book is dedicated:

- The teen PKs of the Prairie Lakes District, scattered across the fields and forests of Minnesota, in the region where our service to teen PKs first began. This amazing group of people—Missy and Mindy, Naomi and Nicole, Ginger and Jeffrey, PJ and Zach, Rebecca and Melinda, Luke and Sarah, Kathleen, and more—became an extended family to us. When David's brother died suddenly—just before our third annual retreat with this group—we almost canceled our speaking and serving. Instead, we went ahead with the retreat, during which we received much more ministry than we provided. We have never in our lives felt more loved and accepted, more valued and respected than we did among our friends here. We are forever grateful, and these amazing men and women are forever part of our family. We have celebrated their weddings and dedicated their children—our family keeps growing.

- The pastors and partners of the Southeast Europe Region, where we serve and help at an annual conference and retreat. Each year, one of the highlights of our year is to meet with this group, work with this group, and learn from this group. Men and women from places like Romania, Bulgaria, Kosovo, Turkey, Poland, and Hungary gather for an annual conference that is part worship, part learning, part counseling, and part celebration. We value being included! We have too many friends among this group to list by name, but for each one of you, we are grateful. We love you, Southeast Europe!

- The many ministry wives who have told us how *Becoming Your Husband's Best Friend* has transformed their marriages. We wrote the book for all wives, not just the wives of those in ministry, but somehow pastors' wives have made this book their favorite. Yes, we know that many women serve in pastoral ministry too—we rejoice with them and we affirm their service. Yet somehow, the role of pastor's wife is even more difficult than the role of pastor. When your husband is criticized or threatened, rejected or harmed, those wounds become personal and powerful. We pray for dozens of ministry wives on a regular basis—you know who you are.

- Turning to pastors themselves—we dedicate this book to Dr. Paul Cunningham, together with his wife, Dr. Connie Cunningham. Paul and Connie serve as an enduring model of husband-and-wife ministry. We learned so much from their teaching and their example! Paul preached in services while Connie taught married couples in her Sunday school classes. Both Paul and Connie have a huge gift for teaching: both of them are brilliant and gifted. Yet beyond the brilliance and the gifts, their personal example is even larger for us. We value their walk with God, their commitment to him and to each other, and their ongoing legacy of fruitful ministry.

- We also joyously dedicate this book to our current pastors and their partners, a team that includes Dr. Larry and Nancy Osborne, Chris and Amy Brown, Charlie and Suzy Bradshaw, J. D. and Linda Larson, and Gary and Sharon Vanderford. Week by week we watch these gifted and creative people serve the growing congregation of North Coast Church in Vista— our home church for more than a decade. These couples model spiritual and relational health, emotional and psychological balance, well-balanced priorities in ministry, great parenting, and more. We count our blessings to know pastors and partners like these, and we are constantly grateful for the wisdom they share. We are better for knowing them!

- Among the pastors who shaped Lisa's life as she was growing up, Lisa would like to mention Wesley Burns, Paul Marshall, and David Figg. Each one was a mentor and example, a leader and friend. Wes Burns remains a close friend to this present day; we value Wes and Zelda and each of their children and grandchildren. What a loving and remarkable family circle! If anyone knows how to raise great kids while coping with the pressures of ministry, it is Wes and Zelda.
- Among the pastors who shaped David's life as he was growing up, David would like to mention Paul McGrady, Howard Borgeson, and Gary Jones. Paul McGrady was a fireball preacher and evangelist. Howard Borgeson was a patient pastor and church builder. Gary and Juanita Jones led the youth group, modeled Christian marriage, counseled many teens, and pointed people toward Christ. Years later, Dr. Gary and Juanita Jones remain among our close friends. We are still learning from Gary and Juanita and their excellent example!

In such a short space it is not possible to mention all those who matter, yet this little list comes from our hearts. This book is dedicated to all pastors and partners, all the children and teens who grow up in a setting of pastoral ministry, whether or not we've met you, whether or not we ever do meet you.

We love you, we pray for you, and we value your service.

May God encourage you today with his nearness and his love.

From the journey—*David & Lisa*

CONTENTS

Foreword   **13**

Section One: The Impact of Stress   **15**

  1. How Stress Affects Us as Persons   17

  2. How Stress Affects Us as Families   35

**Section Two: Five Key Stressors that Impact
Ministry Health and Well-Being**   **51**

  Section Two Introduction   53

  3. Significant Stressor: Role Ambiguity   58

  4. Significant Stressor: Performance Anxiety   83

  5. Significant Stressor: Bivocational Complexity   100

  6. Significant Stressor: Financial Scarcity   115

  7. Significant Stressor: Situational Adversity   129

**Section Three: Strategies that Can Reduce
Ministerial Stress**   **147**

  Section Three Introduction   149

  8. Five Secrets of Stress-Resistant Pastors   151

  9. Coping Mechanisms: Four Habits that Can
     Lower Your Stress   169

About the Authors   **181**

Notes   **185**

FOREWORD

For much of my life and ministry, God has kept me busy as a "pastor to pastors," helping those who serve in roles of ministry and leadership. I have spoken to pastors and listened to pastors. I have counseled with ministers and prayed with ministers. These great men and women have come to mean a lot to me—their burdens have been my burdens; their concerns have been my concerns.

In my role at Focus on the Family and in other settings, I have seen the great stresses that are faced by those who serve in ministry. There are almost too many to mention here—time management, financial stress, physical and/or emotional burnout, dysfunction within the church. On top of that, there are often pressures or expectations from the denomination or perhaps the church board. There is far too much criticism of pastors, and there is far too little support.

It is not surprising that so many leave the ministry, but it is surely sad. Faced with pressures and stresses in their marriage and family, in their career and employment, in their personal sense of self-worth and success, pastors leave the ministry at an alarming rate. I do not blame them; I weep for them and with them.

As I prepared to write the foreword for this new book, a study crossed my desk that reports more than 1,700 pastors leave the ministry each month. Each one of these pastors has a story. Each one of these pastors probably felt a sense of divine calling when he or she entered the ministry.

What can we do to support those who serve? How can we do a better job of helping them overcome their many stresses? How can we help them succeed?

With these questions in mind, it is a joy to introduce you to this new book, written by Dr. David and Lisa Frisbie. David and Lisa serve as coordinators of Marriage and Family Ministries for the global Church of the Nazarene, yet their serving and helping takes them to churches of many denominations and places.

David and Lisa have a heart for serving and helping. Each year they speak at Ministers and Mates Retreats, present workshops and seminars for pastors and their families, and serve those in ministry in a wide variety of ways. Out of their ministry and experience—so far—have come more than twenty books about marriage and family life.

This new book, published by Beacon Hill Press of Kansas City, arrives to help and support those who serve in pastoral ministry. It arrives to help them thrive in their marriages, experience good health in their family circles, and redefine what success in ministry looks like and feels like. This book arrives to bring light and life.

Although no single book can solve all the challenges of ministry, my prayer is that this book will help many pastors and spouses find fresh hope, discover new tools for coping with stress, and move forward to more effective life and ministry. May God help us to "serve those who serve" in every good way.

—Dr. H. B. London

SECTION ONE
THE IMPACT OF STRESS

1
HOW STRESS AFFECTS US AS PERSONS

After serving almost five years in a difficult and conflicted pastoral setting, Allen knew he needed to make a change. His heart for ministry, always at the core of his personal identity, was beating very faintly. His love for God, usually among his primary passions, didn't feel intense or strong. Week after week, Allen dreaded the arrival of Sunday mornings. He grew tired of standing in the pulpit trying to preach God's truth to people who either didn't pay attention to him or simply didn't care.

In the downward spiral of disappointment and disillusionment, Allen lost his energy, worried about his performance in the pulpit, and began to wonder if he had misunderstood the divine call. Sometimes in his weaker moments, Allen even considered whether he had completely lost his faith.

"I didn't feel anything at all," Allen remembers. "I didn't feel close to God, and sometimes I wondered if God was listening to my prayers. I didn't feel like I could trust anybody in the congregation. In the midst of all that, my strongest supporter on the church board resigned suddenly, without telling me in advance. He also withdrew from all his ministry roles in the church, leaving some huge gaps for us. My kids could see that I was struggling, my wife knew that I was struggling, and I realized that I was struggling, but I couldn't see any real solution to the problems. I felt like I was drowning or suffocating, but slowly.

"I had been trying for months to get a new assignment elsewhere. I had called a few district superintendents, brushed up my résumé, and talked to other pastors at conferences and conventions. Everyone knew I was looking to make a change, but no doors opened up for me. Every once in a while something seemed like a good prospect, but somehow my name never got to the top of the stack.

"One day I realized that doors weren't going to open for me, so I needed to make a new plan. I called my dad, who was still on the family farm where I grew up. It was early spring, and he was getting ready to work the fields. I asked him if my family and I could move there. I asked him if he would let me help him with tilling and planting and tending the crops, if we could live there and I could work through the summer until harvesttime. I hoped that by harvesttime I could figure out what to do next."

Allen's father welcomed the help, realizing that his son was struggling to find his way. So on a crisp spring morning in the upper Midwest, Allen resigned his pastorate, gave two weeks' notice, and made plans to move south with his family. The congregation seemed surprised by Allen's abrupt announcement, but no one made any effort to change his mind or to persuade him to stay.

A mere seventeen days after he submitted his resignation, Allen arrived and unpacked at his parents' farm. He and his family moved into a mobile home near the old barn and prepared to spend a few months living there, doing temporary work. The sudden move was a huge change for everyone. Allen recalls worrying about how his wife and children would react to the new reality.

"I felt like a failure," Allen tells us over coffee and muffins. "I felt like everyone saw me as a failure, like everyone knew I was a failure. Plus I hadn't just failed in a business or in my career—I had failed

God himself. I had failed in my spiritual duties. I had failed in my calling. I was at low tide in every part of my life, the lowest I had ever been. I was sick, tired, overweight, and stressed out. I felt defeated in every sense of the word, like I couldn't do anything right.

"If my dad hadn't let us come there and live on the farm, I don't know where I'd be right now. I don't know what else we could have done."

Removing the Stressors

By God's grace, farm life was invigorating—right from the start.

Within a month of arriving in the new setting, Allen was sleeping better than he had slept in years. He was losing weight without making any noticeable changes to his diet. If anything, Allen notes, he was probably eating more food, more often, than he did before. Yet the excess weight was dropping away rapidly, and Allen was sleeping all night long on a regular basis.

"I hadn't slept well in years, basically the whole time we served at [name of former church]. I had gained thirty or forty pounds in five years of ministry there, mostly from using food as therapy. I would come home from a board meeting or from spending time with a difficult person, and I would eat some food to calm down. Even if it was nine or ten o'clock at night, I would make myself a huge meal and just eat. Eating was about the only vice I allowed myself—I always felt a little better after a snack or a big meal."

While serving as a pastor in a conflicted church, Allen had slept poorly, gained weight, and experienced frequent bouts of cold and flu.

"I was sick a lot," Allen says in describing that season in his life. "I didn't blame my sickness on the church—it wasn't the fault of the congregation—but looking back I never realized how often I was sick with colds or flu or sore throats or some combination of that."

While feeling like a failure or when returning from a difficult conversation, Allen had used food as his therapy—feeling a bit better in the moment, yet adding even more pounds to his already-overweight physique. He was eating too much, sleeping too little, and coping with near constant bouts of physical illness.

Allen was a poster child for stress disease, a living example of the ways that prolonged stress can impact our physical and emotional health. The more time he invested in a conflicted and challenging situation, the more stressed he became. Allen was trapped in a vicious cycle of conflict, stress, and poor health.

Then a move to the farm changed all of that, almost from the beginning.

"For one thing, I slept all night long," Allen says with a grin. "I slept like a baby at night. We were living in a trailer, with most of our furniture and clothes stored in a nearby barn. You wouldn't think I would sleep well at all under those conditions, but I slept great. We had our two young sons sleeping on bunk beds in a tiny room, but even they seemed to sleep well after we got to the farm.

"Things were so quiet at night, so different from our life in the city. We didn't have a phone in the trailer. I had a cell phone, of course, but I got in the habit of just turning it off at night. Who was going to call me? I wasn't on duty anymore; I wasn't anybody's pastor. If my parents needed me for an emergency, they were just a few hundred yards away in the main house. So I just shut my phone off at night.

"I started sleeping like a rock," Allen sighs. "Maybe for the first time in my life, or at least for the first time since seminary. I wasn't on call, nobody was depending on me; there just wasn't any reason to be tense at night when I laid down to sleep. Plus, I was exhausted from working the fields all day or repairing a broken fence. I got in the habit of coming back to the trailer about sunset, having a big meal with my family, and then just playing with my kids for a while. After an hour or so of running around with my boys, I was so tired that I could sleep through anything."

Allen started sleeping well, losing weight, and feeling better about his life. It was perhaps a month or so before he noticed that there was a new spring in his step, a frequent smile on his face, and a lot more relaxation in his schedule—despite his busy days of physical labor on a working farm.

"My wife looked at me one night as we ate dinner," Allen said, smiling, "and she grinned and told me I was a new man. Until she said that, I hadn't been paying attention. I was just taking one day at a time, enjoying the outdoor work and loving the fact that I had a lot more time with my kids. All of a sudden, when my wife told me I was a new man, I realized how much my life had changed—for the better."

Stress and Physical Health

Looking back at Allen's experience from a safe clinical distance, we can watch as he moves from a high-stress environment into a context with much less stress—and we can track significant changes in his physical health, emotional responses, and overall wellness. These differences are visible and quantifiable in several major categories. It becomes clear that there were negative physical changes in Allen during his pastoral ministry, while he was dealing with stress factors in his daily life. Later, there were positive physical changes when his stress levels decreased as he moved to the family farm.

We watch stress impact Allen through five years of difficult life in ministry, as Allen gains weight, loses sleep, and experiences frequent illness. Then as Allen removes himself from most of the stressors in his environment, we watch again as quite different physical changes develop and emerge. Allen begins to sleep better, starts to lose his excess weight, and is described by his wife as a new man.

With Allen's case as a backdrop, let's look at the way stress affects physical health and well-being. We'll discover that our stress can be positive or negative, and that either way, our body moves through much the same cycle in response.

Positive stress, which is called *eustress*, describes the way our bodies respond to external stimulation, such as cheering for our daughter's soccer team when she scores a key goal or her team wins a game. We are excited and "buzzed"—our physical bodies respond in a variety of ways, which we'll discuss soon. This is a form of stress to our physical systems, even though the stimulus or trigger event is positive. Eustress might also describe our response when we begin dating a new person, caught up in a rush of hormones as we experience attraction or arousal.

Most of us would not consider a soccer victory or a new relationship to be "stressful," yet, in fact, our bodies experience significant stress in these situations. Because the stress is essentially positive, the term *eustress* is used to describe it.

Some of our physiological responses during eustress—an accelerated heartbeat, times of rapid or shallow breathing, a sudden burst of adrenaline—are identical to our body's responses during times of negative stress. From our body's perspective, in terms of physical responses and cycles, stress is stress.

When stress is a response to negative conditions or factors, the proper term to describe the situation is *distress*. In common usage, many people use the term *stress* when what they are experiencing is actually *distress*. Most people don't describe scoring a soccer goal, dating a new person, or winning a big game as being "stressful." For the purposes of this book, as we will make clear in later sections and chapters, we will mostly use the term *stress* in a way that would be more clearly understood, from a clinical perspective, to be *distress*.

In either case—eustress or distress—our body's response is similar. We experience a range of physical reactions to what begins as either a mental or physical stimulus or trigger event. We begin a cycle of stress response that is predictable and observable.

There are three primary stages of our body's response to instances of stress. While the situations or issues can vary, our body essentially moves through each of these three phases when confronting a stressful event or experience.

Here is a quick, simple overview of the three stages:

1. **Trigger event or stimulus.** Our body alerts us to something that needs our immediate and specific attention. For example, if we happen to step on a thorn, a sharp pain stabs at us and demands that we notice and resolve the problem. The purpose of the pain is to alert us to the issue and to elicit an appropriate reaction, such as taking our foot off the thorn and bandaging the wound. Without the trigger event, our body might not notice a serious threat or a looming problem. Some who write about stress call this trigger event an alarm or an onset. Perhaps the term *detonator* might also be appropriate. Something explodes or erupts so that we pay attention, notice the problem, and respond appropriately.

2. **Response or resolution.** Our body releases essential hormones that speed up our reaction to the problem or issue. Adrenaline, one of two key hormones released in response to stress, sets us up for a "fight or flight" reaction to the stressor. For the purposes of understanding this cycle, think of adrenaline as being similar to a jolt of caffeine—as if your body, making up its own mind on the matter, grabs an extra-large energy drink and slams it down fast. Adrenaline gives you a "rush" of extra energy and extra speed so that you can respond to the threat or the trigger. In our daily lives, as we cope with the small and large crises that occur during a busy day, many of us receive these sudden jolts of adrenaline. The release of adrenaline into our system helps us move faster, be more decisive, and move forward with clarity.

3. **Recovery phase.** Having faced the threat and dealt with the problem, our entire physical system needs time to repair, recuperate, and recover. This is the body's "downtime" to restore health and vitality to all of its systems. As you might guess from the term and this brief description, sleep or rest

is a major part of the recovery phase. Your body's physical health and well-being depends on getting enough sleep and receiving enough rest. Without rest, the body cannot repair itself properly. During this phase there is a general "letdown" of energy and enthusiasm, which is often accompanied by a feeling of slight or general depression. This phase of our stress response is very similar to what happens when our body winds down from the "buzz" of a highly caffeinated energy drink or multiple cups of coffee. We enjoy the sharpness of the buzz, but we also realize that an eventual letdown will occur. In terms of our response to stress, this letdown is a necessary and essential part of our wellness.

Whether the stress in question is positive or negative, our body responds in the same way, working through all three of the phases we have just discussed above. For example, as you watch your daughter score a key soccer goal, you leap up in the stands, raise your arms high above your head, and scream out loud, yelling her name. You're excited and everyone knows it!

There has been a trigger event (goal!) and now there is a response (jump; cheer). As your cheer subsides and you return to your seat, your body begins a recovery phase in order to stabilize your system. Thankfully, soccer goals don't happen continuously. If they did, your body would be under constant stress, despite the "happy" reason for it. In the aftermath of an adrenaline jolt, your body needs time to recover and recharge—and happily, most youth soccer games allow plenty of time for this to occur.

When our daughter's soccer team scores a goal, most of us don't think of this as being a "stressful" event. Yet our bodies are responding with exactly the same cycles and system as if we had suddenly met a bear in the woods or accidentally stepped on a sharp tack we didn't see. First there is a trigger event; then, there is an accelerated reaction or response, and after our response subsides there is a tangible hormone lag as our body takes steps to recover, recuperate, and restore. This letdown or lag is vital to our overall health and well-being.

Adrenaline Junkies

Type A personalities, always striving and achieving, might be described as consciously or unconsciously seeking out "trigger" events in order to sustain the rush of their physical response systems. Some observers have talked about Type A persons as being "adrenaline junkies," and this term may be apt in its description. Type A personalities do, in fact, have a constant flood of adrenaline in their systems, often overwhelming the body and depriving it of sufficient time to recover. This is why phrases like "burnout" can apply to Type A's at a later stage, and why physical ailments such as heart disease or stroke often befall a driven, Type-A adult.

Too much adrenaline is a harmful thing. It turns out that your mom was right all those years ago when she insisted that you get enough sleep. Mom knew that your body needs rest in order to fully recover and fully protect you from future threats. Your immune system—your body's primary line of defense against unwanted invaders—depends on the recovery phase in order to function properly. When you deprive yourself of adequate recovery time, your immune system is weakened. And when your immune system is weakened, your body is more vulnerable to threats such as germs, disease, and chronic or terminal illnesses.

We need not be a Type A personality in order to be at risk for stress disease. All of us, if facing prolonged stress or unresolved issues, are impacted by the changes in physical health that result from overextending the response phase. Simply stated, our bodies are not designed to experience extended seasons of ongoing stress. Instead, our systems are designed to protect us from occasional stress, the surprises of daily living, and the chance encounters we have as we go about our daily business and family life.

Modern lifestyles, particularly in Western cultures, have the effect of exposing us to extended periods of stress. Unknowingly, we overdose on the response phase while never fully experiencing enough restoration and recovery. The result of this consistent and systemic exposure to ongoing stress is a breakdown in health, both individually (microcosm) and in our society (macrocosm). Western society is beset by a wide range of illnesses and diseases that can be traced or linked to stress—especially prolonged, unresolved, ongoing distress. Increasingly, as Western ways impact other cultures and civilizations, the diseases of modern life are impacting even the more remote reaches of our spinning planet.

Physical Responses to Stress (Bodily Systems)

The onset of stress (trigger event or alarm) sets in motion a wide range of changes in our body's physical systems. Listed below are some of the ways that our body's systems are impacted by a stressful situation or environment:

Brain. As our brain processes the signals that trigger a stress response, there is an increase in blood flow to our brain cells. We may feel more energized or mentally alert. We may believe that we can "think better" or "think more clearly." In reality, our mental processes are no better or worse than before—they are simply being sped up or accelerated by the onset of increased blood flow.

There is a reverse of this process when we eat a big meal, and there is a resultant increase in blood flow to our digestive system. This inevitably causes us to feel sluggish or like we are "thinking less clearly" when in reality, this is once again a matter of simple physics. More blood flowing to the brain increases our awareness and heightens our experience of thinking, choosing, and deciding. Less blood flowing to the brain has the opposite effect—we may feel inclined to take a nap, believing that our mental processes have turned to sludge.

Lungs. There is often a breathing response to stressful triggers. There may be an initial sharp intake of breath, or we may begin breathing more rapidly. As this response occurs, we are also receiving an increase of blood flow to the lungs. The increase of blood flow increases the amount of oxygen available via our blood. Oxygen energizes us and activates a higher level of functioning. At the same time, our lungs are expelling harmful emissions at a faster rate, clearing our systems. There is an uptake in oxygen received and a quickening of the expulsion process for other unhelpful substances.

If, for example, we are going to run away from danger (fight or flight), our lungs will need the extra capacity in order to fuel our running. So the brain begins to signal to increase blood flow to the lungs and also may signal the lungs to breathe more rapidly, setting off a two-pronged approach to increasing the amount of oxygen that is available for our lungs to process. Result: more energy that the body can use to successfully respond to the stressor.

Heart. As you might expect, given the fact that blood flow increases to the brain and to the lungs, your heart is working harder. Almost immediately, your heart moves into high-alert status, raising your blood pressure and speeding your pulse. This response is not dangerous to the heart when it happens in small doses, or in occasional responses to stress. Your heart was designed to function in exactly this way—even if caught by surprise, your heart can quickly ramp up your pulse rate and blood pressure, rushing needed blood and oxygen to your brain and body.

Yet when the heart is asked to function this way for an extended period of time, or when blood pressure is raised for a long time, a wide range of dysfunction can and does occur. We will say more about this in the following section. For now, it is enough to know that the heart responds to stress by speeding up and/or by increasing the blood pressure toward the same purpose (faster response). These are normal and natural heart functions and these functions occur by design. It is only when these functions are overused, or the heart is overtaxed, that a wide range of difficult health issues come into play.

Muscles. It's no illusion: in the moment of sudden need, the rush of blood to our muscles actually does increase our strength. This may explain, at least in part, the anecdotal stories about someone lifting a fallen tree limb or a heavy car so that a friend or family member (or fellow soldier) can escape certain disaster. While under normal circumstances, a person would not have enough strength for this task, the body's stress response makes it possible by rushing extra blood to the muscles, including an extra supply of oxygen via the blood system.

If we are surprised by a sudden threat and we need to run away, our muscles receive an extra boost to make this possible. This is why we may be able to run long distances, or for extended periods of time, when we are responding to a perceived threat. In "real life," our slow speed would doom us to be mauled by the bear or captured by the person chasing us. Yet due to our body's stress response and the increased flow of blood to our muscles, we may get an extra boost that lets us escape, run away, find safety, and survive.

Once again, this is exactly how our bodies are designed to function. Yet also once again, we are not meant to be constantly running, constantly evading capture, or constantly rushing away from angry bears in the woods. Our body's defense systems are designed to get us some quick help in urgent situations, not for coping with extended seasons of nothing but flight or escape. Eventually—or in some cases fairly quickly—we reach our limits and "hit the wall" in terms of our body's ability to evade or flee.

Stomach. A rush of excess acid reaches our digestive systems as we respond to a stressful encounter. The purpose of this acid boost is to speed up our digestive system. Again, if our need is for escape or flight, our body needs to be done with digestion so that maximum energy is available to us as we flee.

Excess acid, or some form of gastrointestinal distress, is one of the most-reported symptoms of stress. We may or may not be aware of changes in our breathing or even our pulse, but if we get heart-burn—that, we notice. This symptom is at or near the top of any list of self-reported symptoms of stress. Related issues include acid re-flux, ulcers, bloating, gas, and a host of symptoms that stressed-out workers experience frequently.

Harmful or Helpful: It's a Question of Degree

As we review the ways in which our body responds to stress, it's clear that the purpose of each response is to provide us with the energy and alertness we need in order to avoid harm or danger. Our stress-response systems are in place for a reason—in times of emergency, we need the extra boost that our rapid heart rate, oxygenated blood, and stronger muscles can provide.

Simply put, our stress-response system isn't bad—it is very, very good.

The problem is that we are not designed or intended to live in constant stress and under ongoing duress. When the body's stress-response system is triggered over and over again, and the stress-response system responds exactly as it is designed to, the same chemistry that usually helps us becomes an enemy of our health.

A little adrenaline for a sudden emergency is a very good thing. A constant rush of adrenaline through our systems leads to a wide range of ailments, including cholesterol damage. Although reporting on heart conditions and cardiac disease often mentions cholesterol and statins, there is not enough reporting on the linkage between high levels of adrenaline and the many kinds of damage that choles-terol can do.

An ample body of evidence confirms that having a high level of adrenaline in your system contributes to having higher levels of LDLs—low density lipoproteins—which have a harmful impact on heart health. If you've had your cholesterol checked recently (and if you haven't, you should), you know that you received two numbers in the rating—one number for HDLs (high-density lipoproteins) and the other number for LDLs.

Having higher levels of HDLs appears to offer some protection against the prospect and impact of heart disease. Having higher levels of LDLs appears to be a risk factor of critical importance. What's missing from this conversation is the reality that high levels of adrenaline are implicated in higher levels of LDLs.

Here's another way of thinking about all of this.

Your body was designed with an intricate, helpful emergency-response system that protects you in a time of danger. Although it's somewhat of an exaggeration, your emergency-response system can give you "warp speed" or "superhuman strength" in times of crisis or emergency. Nearly every major system in your body is designed to be able to function at a higher state of alert and to produce impressive results in performance.

Yet your body was never designed to live in "panic mode" on a regular basis. The whole point of an emergency-response system is to respond to emergencies. Instead, modern life creates "emergency" conditions on a regular basis. When you live in a continuous state or season of stress, you tax and overload your body's natural line of defense against disease and poor health.

In the case of our body's emergency-response system, too much of a good thing is definitely a bad thing. Our body's emergency-response system was designed to be helpful occasionally—when needed. It was not designed to be permanently in the "on" position—constantly juicing us with adrenaline or cortisol, constantly revving up our blood pressure, breathing, or energy levels.

Many of the diseases and ailments of modern life can be traced to an overfunctioning of our body's stress-response systems, with the result that our immune systems are weakened, our body chemistry is impacted negatively, and our health suffers accordingly. We experience cardiovascular, respiratory, and digestive issues and problems that are a direct result of our overtaxed, overfunctioning stress-response systems.

From heart disease to liver conditions, from cancer to coronaries, an increasing body of evidence implicates stress and the body's natural response to it as a contributing factor to many of our most prevalent health problems.

Treating the Symptoms—Not the Causes

As we look back at the various ways our body is impacted by stress, it's interesting to note how many modern remedies target the symptoms of these issues without treating or responding to the underlying causes. We notice the symptoms, complain about the symptoms—and in response an army of medical researchers goes to work trying to treat or mitigate the symptoms with a new "miracle drug."

Got gastric distress? Pop an antacid. Planning to eat an unhealthy, unwise meal in the near future? Swallow a prescription antacid prior to dining. Advances in medicine and medical technology allow us to treat many of the troubling symptoms of modern life while continuing to make many of the lifestyle and dietary mistakes that are staples of our modern lifestyles. We like our mistakes, and we plan to keep right on making them. Please pass the pills.

Got a headache? We have pain relievers for that—generic, brand name, and prescription. Aches and pains throughout your body can be targeted with very specific analgesics and pain relievers that mitigate your symptoms—while doing nothing at all about the underlying causes. Thanks to these miracle medicines, we can literally "get on with life" while a pharmaceutical breakthrough helps us mostly ignore our symptoms. Back to work; we are feeling better and no longer distracted by our pressing ailments and pains.

Ah, relief. Now—where was I?

Our bodies must be highly confused by all of this. Our bodies are busy triggering our stress-response systems while we blatantly ignore the warnings and simply pop more pills. The more loudly our body speaks to us about our high levels of stress, the more often we dissolve a fizzy remedy in a glass of water or reach for a capsule or a tablet. We hear the warning, but we rush to treat the symptom instead of stopping to diagnose or understand the root problem.

There is nothing wrong with these amazing, often-used remedies—they help us feel better and get back to work. Yet the underlying problems we face remain unaddressed and unresolved. While Western and Eastern nations rush to accomplish more, achieve more, and succeed in a highly complex and competitive marketplace, personal and individual health suffers. Trapped in a vicious cycle, we work harder, medicate more, and put even more strain on the very systems that were designed to guard our health—not to attack it.

How much of the strain on our health-care system could be alleviated if we would stop, look, and listen to the many ways our body tries to alert us to danger? As the writer of Psalms observed, we are "fearfully and wonderfully made" (Psalm 139:14), and part of that intricate design is a stress-response system that alerts us to problems so that we can take appropriate actions.

All too often, instead of learning from our stress and taking wise actions to correct the issues, we simply medicate the symptoms of our stress so that we can go right back to the behaviors, anxieties, and choices that put stress in our lives. At some point, perhaps our Creator might wonder whether we've noticed that, among his other gifts to us, he gave us brains—hoping we might use them.

Lessons from Allen

Allen, who fled the pastoral ministry to till the fields of his father's farm, learned a wide range of lessons as he watched himself regain physical health. Along with the physical changes he experienced,

Allen noticed that his emotions were rebounding. He was laughing more loudly and more often. Instead of anxious thoughts flooding his mind as he began each day or as he attempted to fall asleep, Allen found himself surrounded by a calm and tranquil environment that soothed his nerves and restored his composure.

Allen's stress began to ebb and recede.

His body and spirit began an extended season of recovery.

"He leads me beside the still waters. He restores my soul" (Psalm 23:2-3, NKJV) is how the Psalmist describes this process. Once again, the wisdom of the divine Creator is much in view. It is not good for persons—including pastors—to live with so much tension and anxiety, constantly engaged in conflicted and challenging situations. The toll on the pastor's health, which may also include damage to the pastor's marriage and family, is too great. God's design is not intended to lead us to burnout but to lead us to still waters, calm repose, and the restoration of our souls and spirits.

"I had been ignoring the Sabbath, among my many other sins," Allen says now as he reflects on his pastoral season. "I preached the Ten Commandments but I took some liberties with them, especially God's command that we should honor the Sabbath.

"Although obviously Sunday could not have been a Sabbath for me, I believe God intended for me to have another full day as Sabbath rest, and I never really tried to achieve that," Allen admits. "I believed that if I tried harder, worked harder, and kept on trying to resolve the issues, things would get better. Instead, what actually happened was that my own health kept getting worse.

"I was losing my perspective about God, about pastoral ministry, about the worth and value of people, about many things," Allen said, sighing. "I don't know how close I came to having a complete breakdown of some kind, but there were days when I felt pretty close to that. And there were days when I would have welcomed that, quite frankly, because it would have been a way of escape."

Allen's candor points us in helpful directions.

We are "fearfully and wonderfully made," and the design of our body includes a stress-response system that is helpful and good. However, the contours of modern life expose us to stressful situations and challenging personal environments, such as pastoral ministry. If we remain in a state of constant exposure to stressful persons and stressful contexts, we overtax and overactivate our God-given emergency-response systems. The result is an erosion of our personal health, triggered and activated by the very responses that were designed to save us.

Of all the phases and cycles of our body's responses to stress, the "recovery" phase is most often ignored. Yet we ignore this recovery at our own peril. Pushing past any reasonable boundaries, we hit the wall, reach our limits, and begin to break down physically or emotionally. We need the recovery phase just as often as we need the trigger and response phases—each cycle needs its own recovery.

Perhaps this is one of the many reasons why our Creator gave us a Sabbath and then told us he was absolutely serious about how—and how often—we observed it. He placed this instruction in the "Big Ten."

Christ tells us about this in his own analysis of God's design. "The Sabbath was made for man, not man for the Sabbath" (Mark 2:27), Christ explains. In other words, Sabbath rest is not a rule to follow but instead a divine prescription given for our own health and well-being. God gave us the Sabbath so that our bodies and spirits could rest, recover, and be restored.

2
HOW STRESS AFFECTS
US AS FAMILIES

Gary moved his family to a new church assignment just as his only daughter was about to begin her junior year of high school. Daughter Sarah, wise beyond her years at age sixteen, understood her dad's desire to make a move. She felt like she was given a full voice as the family made the choice to move halfway across the country and begin a new ministry.

"I was so proud of her," Gary tells us over muffins and coffee, remembering his daughter's prayers and spiritual process. "My wife and I were pretty solid in our decision, but we knew the move would be hardest on Sarah. We included her in the conversation right from the start. We asked her to pray, and we told her she was a big part of the family and she would be a big part of our decision.

"We meant that. We talked to her, explained things to her, asked her to pray, and then really listened to her. We took things a lot more slowly than we would have if we didn't have kids. She was our only child, and we didn't want to ruin her life by moving at the wrong time or by going to the wrong place.

"Can you understand what that feels like as a father?" Gary asks us.

"Do you realize how serious I was, and how serious my wife was, about wanting our daughter to feel included and valued as we decided to make a move?"

Gary seems on the verge of tears as he remembers his daughter's maturity and spiritual growth while the family considered its choices. He pauses a moment before finding his voice and resuming the narrative.

"Sarah was our only daughter, and moving her in the middle of high school seemed like maybe the toughest time to make a move. So we told her she could have a full vote—and we told her if she voted no, we wouldn't move. I honestly don't know if we would have stayed in [prior location] if Sarah voted no, but as it happened we never needed to find out. Sarah prayed a lot. By the time she was finished praying about it, she believed in her heart that God wanted us to move.

"She sat down with us and told us it was okay, that she was sure God was in this, and that she would be fine with the move," Gary says, sniffling. "I've never been so proud of my daughter as I was on that day. She could have stopped us from moving—or at least made us wait a lot longer—but there she was, praying about it and getting her own sense of direction from God.

"How cool is that?" Gary wonders aloud. "My daughter was only in high school, but she was already learning how to listen for God's voice when it was time to make a major decision. I was so proud of her."

The family prayed together, decided together, and moved together.

Even so, the move proved to be more challenging than any of them had realized as they prayed about making the change.

"Our new church had no youth group," Gary frowns. "And we knew that. It's not like we got there and it was a big surprise. We knew as we visited and met the congregation that the church didn't have a youth group.

"Sarah knew that. My wife and I knew that. The absence of a teen group for Sarah was a big deal for us, and we prayed about that. And even Sarah told us that she thought God was going to bring her some new friends. I remember her telling us that maybe her new friends wouldn't be in our church, but they would still be good Christians, and they would still be good friends."

Gary pauses.

"Can you hear how mature that is for a sixteen-year-old?" he wants to know.

The family arrived at a church with no youth group. As it happened, they arrived in their new town in August, a few weeks before school began.

"Perfect timing," Gary says about the move. "Sarah didn't have to start the school year one place, then catch up somewhere else. She started her junior year of high school with everyone else. She was there on the first day of school."

Sarah, who had been a cheerleader at her previous school, met friends who were trying out for the cheer squad at her new school. Three of them—all juniors, all Christians—connected during fourth hour on the first day of school. From class, they went to lunch period together. A "forever friendship" was born among the three.

"All God," Gary sighs as he recalls the first day of school. "I'm not sure my wife and I did anything except pray that day. We were so wrapped up in Sarah getting off to a good start and making the right kinds of friends. My wife and I both skipped our lunch that day and spent the time praying for our daughter. Sarah didn't know that at the time, and she still doesn't know it. But we were praying for her all day, and we skipped lunch to pray, and we just poured our hearts out to God, asking him to find Sarah some good solid friends."

Gary's prayers were answered.

"She came home from school chattering about tryouts for cheer squad, about her two new friends, about how well school had gone,"

Gary grins. "My wife and I just looked at each other, and I think our faith in God grew by about a thousand percent. I mean, we had prayed all day, asking God for just exactly that kind of miracle, you know? But somehow we were still surprised when God answered. We were still amazed when God did exactly what we asked him to do—or maybe he even went beyond our prayers.

"It was a pretty cool first day of school for the love of our lives," Gary says. "My wife and I kind of cried ourselves to sleep that night—but they were happy tears. We were both praying out loud in our bedroom, just praising God and thanking him for being so good to Sarah. We fell asleep praising God for his goodness."

Sarah's place in the new school was solid and assured. With two new friends beside her, Sarah tried out for cheerleading, dusted off her violin (both of her friends were in the school orchestra), and quickly made friends at lunch hour and beyond.

"She came home from school one day, maybe about the second or third week of classes, and she told us how glad she was that we moved," Gary smiles. "She thanked us for moving and for having faith that God would supply all our needs. She told us she was happier in her new school than she would have been if we had stayed behind and she had kept all her old friends."

Yet the family's joy became the congregation's "concern" in only a few short months. Somehow, the miracle God provided became a sticking point for some of the board members, and through them, the rest of the power structure in the small congregation.

Sarah, with the full approval of her parents, began attending teen group activities with her two new friends, both of whom attended a large and thriving Lutheran church a few miles out of town.

"About half of the kids in her school went to that church," Gary estimates. "Or at least it seemed that way. They had a junior-high pastor and a senior-high pastor and a full calendar of youth activities every week. It was amazing—the kind of thing that larger churches with larger budgets are able to do.

"When Sarah talked to us about going to some of their youth events, we were immediately glad. What parent wouldn't be excited about that? Our church didn't have a youth group—Sarah was literally the only high school student in the entire congregation at that time. So when she asked us about going to youth events with her friends from the Lutheran church, we had absolutely no reservations about it. In fact, we were almost as excited as she was!"

Sarah began attending youth events at the Lutheran church. On Sunday mornings she attended the church where her dad was pastor, sitting with her mother on the second row, piano side. Sarah not only attended Sunday worship with her family but also volunteered to take a monthly turn working in the church nursery. She enjoyed the chance to work with children, and she understood that in a smaller church, everyone needs to pitch in and help.

"She was completely involved in our church," Gary insists. "She sat with her mom every Sunday morning, and she volunteered in the nursery. When we had special events like revival services or workdays at the church, she was there. Sarah demonstrated in every possible way that she was an active part of our local church. She couldn't have participated more or been more visible!"

Somehow, though, word of Sarah's attendance of Lutheran youth events made its way to the chairman of the church board, who was also the patriarch of several interconnected families who controlled the church. News that the pastor's daughter was "involved elsewhere" quickly became a staple of church gossip and a matter of intense church anxiety and concern.

"The church board met to discuss it without even telling me." Gary shrugs, with a look of complete bewilderment on his face. "They met behind my back! And the 'sin' they were discussing was that my Christian teen daughter was attending Christian teen events with her Christian teen friends.

"That's a *problem?*" Gary asks, incredulously. "That's a reason to call a special meeting of the board?"

His rhetorical question hangs in space for a moment.

Gary readily admits that he became defensive when the board surprised him in the next meeting. Without telling him in advance, the chairman of the board began reading a letter—on behalf of the entire board—essentially telling the pastor what to do about his daughter's "problem."

In Gary's own words, he didn't merely get defensive, he got angry.

"I was really mad," Gary allows. "Probably as angry as I've ever been in a church board meeting session. I didn't know this was happening and didn't have any time to prepare a response—they just surprised me with it. And the whole thing had been discussed in a meeting I wasn't even invited to!

"Basically, the letter told me that it was unacceptable for my daughter to be involved with another church, that it was a 'poor reflection on my ministry' that this was happening, and that I needed to instruct my daughter to quit attending this other church with her friends. I needed to 'learn how to manage my own household' is exactly what the board's letter said.

"Also, the letter went on to say that if I failed to take action, it would lead to 'serious consequences for my pastoral ministry' in the days ahead.

"Can you believe that? I mean, were they threatening to cut my salary in half, or fire me, or what?" Gary queries. "They didn't spell it out. They just said that if I didn't obey their orders, there would be 'serious consequences' for my ministry."

Gary sags back in his chair with a long and expressive sigh.

"I was mad," says the ordained minister. "And frankly, if you put me right back into that situation again, I would be mad all over again. I think I could have handled it better, and maybe controlled my speaking better, but the bottom line is: I was mad. And I think everybody in the room could see that."

Gary went home and told his wife, who was even angrier than Gary.

"They have absolutely no right!" Gary's wife insisted. "She is our daughter, not theirs. She is our responsibility, not theirs! This isn't even about her going to a Christian youth group—this is about who gets to raise my daughter!"

From among hundreds of cases we've witnessed, we select Gary's family for this chapter because his situation exemplifies how stress can impact a family while the husband or wife serves in pastoral ministry. One moment a family is united and praising God for his goodness—Christian friends and godly influences for their child—and in the next moment that same family is being attacked by its primary employer for the very same reason—a Christian teen attending a Christian youth group event. Without specific threats being made, there is a general threat of impending economic doom or perhaps the loss of employment altogether.

We'll return to Gary's case after taking a look at how stress impacts a family, with input from recent studies and scientific perspectives. In this next section, we'll take a brief look at the evolution of family stress theory, learning concepts and ideas that we will then (in later chapters) apply to the setting of pastoral ministry.

Family Stress Theory

Our scientific literature regarding family stress theory grows out of projects conducted in the first half of the twentieth century. Early researchers looked at the impact of the Great Depression (the late 1920s and following) on family cohesiveness and family stability. Studies from the University of Michigan and from the University of Chicago—both located in the largely rural Midwestern United States—looked at family stress by examining case studies of specific families.

Although the terminology has evolved and the paradigms of stress theory have shifted several times, this early work remains important to an understanding of family stress and family reactions. Researchers from both universities used the Great Depression as the crisis (we would now say "stressor") and then studied how families responded to severe economic disaster. Some families came through the process fairly well; others suffered immensely. Early researchers included Angell (circa 1936) and Cavan and Ranck (circa 1938), whose contributions to family stress theory remain valuable today.

Angell reported on two significant variables in how a family responded to stress: family integration and family adaptability. *Integration* was Angell's term for "bonds of coherence and unity" within a family—including emotional affection as well as mutual financial and personal support. *Adaptability* reflected a family's shared values as well as their shared flexibility in responding to crisis situations. Angell considered a family's values, such as materialistic vs. nonmaterialistic and responsible vs. irresponsible, while building a profile of an adaptable family. In all, Angell would quantify nine possible family types using his two variables.[1]

Cavan and Ranck approached the problem by evaluating family unity, which they termed "organization." These two researchers looked at the effects of crisis on a family's potential disorganization and reorganization. They found that some families were "well organized," which we might today describe as cohesive or unified. The more organized a family was, the more capable it was of surviving a crisis (stressor) by remaining intact and successful.[2] Again, we might use "unified" here instead of the term "organized" or "well organized." (For related wisdom, see current author Dr. Larry Osborne for his excellent insights on both *Sticky Teams* and *Sticky Church*—books of merit for persons in pastoral ministry.)

Well-organized families, according to Cavan and Ranck, had three common identifying hallmarks or characteristics. These families shared traits such as:

- a high degree of unity
- reciprocal functioning (clear and complementary roles)
- functioning well in their broader community[3]

While these descriptions and characteristics are fairly understandable today, it is worth noting that by "functioning well in their broader community," Cavan and Ranck meant at least these three things:

- being self-supporting or self-sufficient
- being law-abiding and responsible citizens
- getting along well with neighbors (friendly relationships)[4]

Cavan and Ranck were writing in advance of major shifts in U.S. society, promoted during four consecutive Franklin Roosevelt administrations, which would move many individuals and families away from "self-supporting" and in the direction of being supported by federal economic assistance instead. One wonders how these two seminal researchers would react to the idea of a social system built on undermining the basic "organization" of a well-organized family unit, per their own theories and descriptions of the variables in family unity and success.

When the era after World War II ended, family stress theory evolved into a study of family weaknesses or problems that might presage difficulty in responding to stress. Hill (circa 1949; again circa 1958) wrote extensively on responses to stress by family units, primarily looking at indicators of potential weakness that might lead to unsuccessful responses or outcomes. Hill is often called the father of family stress theory, a label that may be unhelpful in its patriarchal implications. He was among the first to write extensively about family stress, using stressors (crisis events or triggers) that were more involved than mere economic setbacks (such as the Great Depression). Hill formulated a system of examining family responses to stress—called the ABCx theory—which remained in wide use for several decades.[5]

A third evolution of family stress theory occurred in the 1980s, with a shift away from looking at potential family weaknesses and searching instead for relevant and shared family strengths. McCubbin and Patterson (1982, 1983 et al.) looked at how well families could cope with stress, based on the presence or absence of these core family strengths.[6] Burr (1989) expanded on these themes with his trifold emphasis on family strengths, methods of coping, and insights from family systems theory.[7]

A fourth evolution in family stress theory is multifaceted and ongoing. Some of the early work in this phase was done by McCubbin and McCubbin (husband and wife; 1991 and 1993). Among other contributions to scientific study, the McCubbinses looked at family *resilience* as a variable in successful responses to stress. The McCubbinses developed the Resiliency Model of Family Stress, Adjustment, and Adaptation, which, despite its cumbersome title, is a useful mechanism for studying how a family responds to success—and why some families adapt and thrive.[8]

Some aspects of this fourth evolution may seem unhelpful to faith-based counselors and those who minister. Much of this fourth-generation theory is rooted in postmodern approaches that are relativistic in nature. The underlying core of this postmodern philosophy is that there is no external or objective reality to be discovered; instead, the meaning and nature of things is revealed by our shared perceptions and understandings. Most in the Christian tradition would favor a more objectivist approach to truth and meaning, yet some of the ideas and concepts of this era in family stress theory—especially resilience—can be useful in examining stress responses and outcomes.

Concluding This Scientific Postscript

From the body of literature that is family stress theory, we will borrow and adapt several core ideas and understandings.

First, we will look at "stressors"—trigger events that were originally called "crises" in the early literature of family stress theory. In the chapters that follow, we will isolate and study some stressors that are endemic to pastoral ministry. Some of these stressors are unique to pastoral service; others may be found in other types of families yet are significantly present in pastoral settings.

Next, we will look at family adaptability and family adjustment as being crucial variables in successful outcomes. Specifically, how can a family become more adaptable (flexible) and in what ways is such flexibility positive and good? Why do some families encounter turbulence while serving in ministry, yet somehow maintain their equilibrium and stability, preserving family unity? What steps might a pastor take toward building an adaptable (and thus successful) family unit?

Finally, we will look at resilience—how some pastoral families are able to survive and thrive despite the reality of harmful people and harmful processes encountered while serving in congregational care. We could fill volume after volume with case studies of "disasters in pastoral ministry," yet that temptation will be avoided here. Instead, we will look at situations and circumstances in which the minister and mate have managed to endure, adjust, recover, and move forward.

In some cases, we will use an unscientific term such as "healing" or "recovery," which can be readily understood in common usage. In many of these cases, we will be describing God's divine intervention and his presence in the midst of our difficulties. In some of these cases, we will be describing family traits or family characteristics that can be learned and acquired, leading to positive outcomes.

But before we go further, let's return to Gary's situation and context and look at how Gary and his family responded to what might be seen as unfair and unwise intervention by a church board.

Stubborn the Elder

With his back to the wall and a veiled threat passed to him in writing, Gary's anger fueled an intense desire to succeed.

"I wanted to win," Gary says today, grimacing. "I wanted to beat these people and show them I could survive their silliness and endure their petty interventions. But even though I wanted to win, I wasn't willing to sacrifice my marriage or cause my daughter any harm in the process. So I really sat down and studied my choices before I made any decisions."

One step Gary took was to contact his district superintendent (DS), who was already aware of the board's consternation. By Gary's memory, his DS was less than supportive of the pastor and the pastor's family.

"Listen," Gary recalls the DS telling him in a lengthy phone call, "whether you like it or not, these people are paying your salary. If you make yourself into their enemy, you're only going to get in worse trouble.

"If you were my son or daughter," the DS continued, "I would advise you to just go along with them, honor their stupid wishes, and get past all this. If they want your daughter to quit attending Lutheran events, then tell her to quit attending the Lutheran events.

"That is a small price to pay for having the support of your church board" is how Gary remembers the parting advice of his presiding administrator.

Gary hung up the phone even angrier than before. Yet he was wise enough not to vent his anger upward (toward the superintendent) or outward (toward the board and its members). Instead, his anger sent him to his knees. Gary prayed and sought divine wisdom for what seemed like an impossible, not to mention unreasonable, situation.

Gary sought input from his wife but hoped to keep his daughter away from all of the trauma and drama. Despite his best efforts to keep her sheltered from the dark side of church politics, Gary's daughter did find out what was going on. Her heart for God and her heart for her parents trumped her other values.

"Dad, it's not that big a deal," Sarah told her pastor and father. "If they want me to quit going to youth nights with my friends, I'll just quit going. It's not worth you losing your job over."

Gary almost cried.

"Honey," he told her, "you're not the problem. The Lutherans are not the problem. Christian youth events are not the problem. Your friends are not the problem."

Wiser than he knew, Gary added an unpremeditated thought.

"Also," he continued, "these people on our church board are not the problem. The real problem is that we have an enemy of our souls, a very real enemy. That enemy just loves to stir up gossip and issues in a church—any church. So try not to resent these people or hate these people—they know not what they do!"

Gary himself admits that he was not wise enough to think of that on his own or mature enough to suggest it on his own.

"I think God just gave me his wisdom in that moment," Gary claims.

After a great deal of thought and prayer, Gary and his wife drafted a simple, one-page response to the church board. Gary asked his wife to accompany him to the next scheduled church board meeting. There, as the first item of business, Gary read his prepared letter, insisting that it be included into the minutes of the board.

Without fanfare and without hyperbole, Gary's letter told the board that he and his wife would be responsible for raising their daughter and that they would raise her to honor Christian values, support Christian causes, and attend Christian events. If some of those events were at other churches, their daughter's attendance would not only be allowed but would be encouraged—now and in the future.

Gary's letter concluded with a powerful summation.

"We are proud of our daughter, and we are proud of her choice to attend Christian youth events that are sponsored by other churches in our community. We are glad that God has a variety of ways to make himself known to Sarah, and we rejoice when Sarah actively and intentionally seeks God's presence.

"We thank God for our daughter, and we thank God for helping us raise her to know him, follow him, honor him, and serve him."

After the reading of the letter, the board was silent. Eventually, other business was conducted. Months went by, and the matter was never raised again in a public session or a board meeting. Gary and his wife received no further letters and were not informed of any further threats against them, either stated or implied.

Sarah graduated from her high school with honors. She and one of her Christian friends both chose the same Christian university, several states away.

With his daughter safely established in a Christian university, Gary began quietly shopping for other ministry opportunities. Having served for several years in his present assignment, Gary accepted a call elsewhere, resigned his pastorate, and moved off the district. Today, Gary is happily serving as the lead pastor of a growing church.

"I'm pretty sure I have forgiven those people," Gary says in talking about the board members of his former congregation. "But I'll tell you the truth—it's a lot easier to forgive them now that I've escaped.

"Pardon my language. But that's exactly how I feel. I feel like I escaped from that place. I feel like my wife and I survived, and our daughter survived—we all survived. We kept going and kept on ministering and we showed them that we weren't going to give in to unreasonable demands.

"But if I was still serving there, would I be able to forgive them and let it go?" Gary asks. He does not answer the question, and perhaps the answer is unknown.

SECTION TWO

FIVE KEY STRESSORS THAT IMPACT MINISTRY HEALTH AND WELL-BEING

INTRODUCTION

Richard drove nearly four hundred miles to be interviewed by a local church board. With the DS present and presiding over the meeting time, Richard recalls that the church board asked him only three questions that night. When it was finally time to present questions to the candidate, the board listed these three topics as their primary concerns. They asked:

1. Do you preach exclusively from the King James Version of the Bible?
2. Do you have any pets?
3. Does your wife play the piano?

Richard recalls wondering why he had wasted so much time driving over. Despite his internal reactions, he smiled and stayed polite. He responded to each person and to each question with diplomacy and tact. He responded to the board's issues calmly, but with a sinking feeling deep in the pit of his stomach. Richard was trying to imagine his wife's reaction when she later learned that the congregation's interest in her was limited to just one question: "Does she play the piano?"

Richard shook his head in bewilderment. In his mind's eye, he could picture his wife responding to that question—whether with anger or laughter he could not be sure. He could hardly wait to discover which it would be.

As he drove home from the interview and processed the experience in prayer, Richard realized that he suddenly had zero interest in becoming the pastor of that local congregation. He also made a mental note to "cross that DS off my list" in searching for future pastoral assignments. If the presiding DS was willing to let a small congregation remain so narrow-minded and controlling, Richard reasoned, it might be wise to avoid serving anywhere on that particular district. Rightly or wrongly, Richard was concerned with the wisdom and maturity of the district leader.

Although he was actively looking for a new assignment and although he genuinely needed the work, Richard wasn't willing to take on a small-minded group that was focused on all the wrong issues. Richard wasn't willing to make the attempt to fit into their narrow, bigoted pastoral profile. He had completed several years of seminary study, including some honors courses in biblical literature, and he could hardly imagine returning to the text and imagery of the King James Version of the Bible now that his insight and knowledge had broadened.

Richard replayed the evening's events in his mind as he drove home. In responding to the board he had tried to understand where the church was coming from with these seemingly crazy questions. For one thing, the previous pastor's large dog had wreaked havoc on the parsonage: hence, the question about whether or not he had a pet. Clearly the board was tired of having the parsonage trashed.

Item two: the previous pastor's wife had played the piano for all of the services; now she was gone. The congregation needed a new accompanist for the worship services: hence, the question about whether his wife played the piano. As he considered the question about the King James Version of the Bible, Richard just shook his head. He thought he might still have a KJV on his iPhone, included among some parallel translations in e-book form. But preaching exclusively from the KJV? Richard didn't know of anyone who did so, and he couldn't imagine trying to limit his biblical inquiry to such a narrow source.

After prayer and reflection (his wife laughed at the piano question) Richard politely withdrew his candidacy. He kept his reasons to himself, only telling the presiding DS that he and his wife "didn't feel called" to allow his name to move forward. Then, out of curiosity, he stayed informed about the church's process. As things developed, it would be ten months before a pastor was located; then the pastor who accepted the role stayed for less than six months before leaving. When that pastor left, Richard informs us, the church was closed and has since been officially disorganized—by a different DS.

✳ ✳ ✳

Allen faced an entirely different challenge during his search for a new pastoral assignment. While interviewing to follow a successful and much-loved church planter, Allen met several times with the members of the church board. During these meetings the DS was present but stayed firmly in the background for most of the conversation and discussions. One particular board member seemed to have the most input in the conversation, and thus perhaps the most control over the interview process and the hiring of the next pastor.

Allen recalls hearing that self-appointed leader make statements that were highly troubling to a prospective minister. He winces a bit at the memories.

"We were sitting around having coffee after that first interview," Allen says, "so everyone had relaxed a bit. The official process was over for the night, and we were sitting around getting acquainted. We were sipping coffee and munching on chocolate chip cookies that the lone female board member had baked and brought to the meeting."

Allen shrugs when we notice the role stereotype—a woman board member baking and serving cookies. "I didn't notice that at the time," Allen admits.

With a smile, he continues his narrative.

"The gentleman who had dominated the discussions that evening made a statement that I will never, ever forget. Without knowing it, he was telling me to avoid this church like the plague. I knew I would never want to serve there."

Allen leans back in his chair and waits a moment before revealing to us exactly what the board member said.

"Here is pretty close to a verbatim," Allen tells us with a wry grin on his face. "The unelected church boss said something like 'When [name of pastor] was here, he controlled everything and decided everything. Since he had founded the church, I guess he thought he could get away with that. Well, I'll tell you something for sure. *We own the ranch now*, and we're going to hire ourselves a ranch hand who will work for us, not the other way around.'"

Allen shakes his head. "I'm pretty sure I've given you the exact quotation," Allen sighs. "He actually said 'we own the ranch' and he actually said 'we are going to hire ourselves a ranch hand.' It's not easy to forget that kind of role-reversed, upside-down thinking about churches and church leadership."

Allen shrugs. "Can you believe that?" he asks us rhetorically. "We own the ranch? Who actually talks like that? Who actually thinks like that?"

Allen's questions are especially relevant to the topic of this book.

In the chapters that follow, we'll consider Allen's experience, Richard's interview, and other cases like these, exploring some of the key specific stressors that one encounters in the setting of pastoral ministry. While perhaps not an exhaustive list, these primary sources of stress emerge in many conversations about the key stress factors faced by today's ministers. We've heard the stress-inducing items on this list mentioned by pastors and spouses in small and large settings, in urban and rural environments, and on four different continents. These issues cross cultures and are repeated to us in a wide range of languages.

As you turn the page and get started, we'll begin with a look at role ambiguity, a stressor that was revealed very clearly in Allen's interview experience.

3
SIGNIFICANT STRESSOR: ROLE AMBIGUITY

So, am I the master or the slave around here?

While few if any pastors would frame the issue with such stark and candid language, this question is at the core of pastoral identity and vocation. Using terms from managerial and corporate worlds: Is the pastor the leader of the congregation, or is the pastor an employee of the congregation?

The currently correct answer—for better or for worse—is "yes." The pastor is both the spiritual leader of the congregation and also a paid staff member who is accountable to a local church board, to whom he relates as employee to employer. Right from the start the relationship of pastor to congregation is clouded by issues of power, control, and ownership. The nature of the relationship is thus ambiguous.

This role ambiguity is a leading stressor of pastors, their spouses, and those who are raised in pastoral homes. When a story is told about a wounded pastor—and when the narrator of the story is the pastor or someone related to the pastor—invariably the wounding or the injustice is rooted in issues of power and control.

"They just didn't treat him right."

"They were really unfair to her."

"She never had a chance there."

These and other phrases are often the beginning of an emotional narrative in which a pastor or minister was voted out, thrown out, or chased out of ministry to a congregation—with or without just cause. Many a perceived injustice begins right here, in this specific pastoral territory. There was a battle over power and control, and someone got hurt during the battle. Often, the damage spreads out in all directions and may affect generations to come.

The Pastor Is Expected to Be the Spiritual Leader

In the stated opinion of many parishioners, the pastor is expected to be the spiritual leader of the whole congregation. This leadership may be exercised poorly or well, but leadership of spiritual matters is generally expected of the pastor and is considered to be one of his or her primary assignments in ministry.

The problem with quantifying and defining spiritual leadership—as opposed to more clear-cut arenas of leadership, such as being a supervisor or manager in a corporation—is that the keys to spiritual leadership are often drawn from one's example and influence, from one's character and virtue, or from one's simplicity and holiness.

If we drew a composite picture of spiritual leadership, it would most likely include some or all of these key ideas, drawn from the observed interior life and personal maturity of the leader in question. Such qualities can be implicit and invisible until a leader lives out his or her life in one place, with one group of people, over a significant period of time. Eugene Peterson has a lovely phrase that might apply to this discussion, which he terms "a long obedience in the same direction."[1] When a leader exhibits a high level of personal character over a long period of time, and does so within a specific and ongoing context, spiritual leadership emerges.

In other words, such leadership and authority is much more relational than positional. It is not about a specific role or place of service but instead is very much about the way in which the life of Christ is made manifest in the person of the leader. This visibility of Christ takes time to emerge, to be seen, and to be trusted.

Simply stated, effective spiritual leadership is drawn from a context in which the minister is known and respected, based on observation and connection over a period of time. No one walks into a new setting as an instantly or immediately effective spiritual leader—unless perhaps he or she is very well known in the broader community. Such exceptions are quite rare.

It is conceivable, for example, that if Billy Graham applied for a local pastoral position in the Dallas metro, he would be the recognized and revered spiritual leader of such a congregation from day one. This would occur because Graham has lived out his simple and authentic Christian faith over a very long period of time, surrounded by a great cloud of witnesses. He has lived a life of integrity and virtue and is honored and respected by those both within and outside of the Christian faith. So perhaps in such a public and identifiable case, a person might have an immediately positive impact as spiritual leader, based on his or her track record in the broader community.

Having said that, it is entirely possible that (were she still living) Mother Teresa might be hired by a local congregation, only to lose her job fairly quickly. One can almost hear the litany of complaints against her being raised in subsequent church board meetings:

"She spends all of her time with the poor and none with us."

"She is ignoring the felt needs of this church."

"She is squandering all of our resources on outsiders."

"I have serious doubts about her theology."

So although Mother Teresa's character and virtue are widely known in the broader community, and although her life is characterized by virtue and simplicity, she might not have immediate effectiveness as a spiritual leader if hired by a local congregation. Her personal holiness, and the direction of her ministry under the guidance of her heavenly Father, might prevent her from being respected as a spiritual leader by a specific church board or congregation. Their aims would be different from hers; their way of quantifying spiritual activity would be different.

Can you see how spiritual leadership is quickly a complex conversation?

In most cases, effective spiritual leadership is earned over time. It does not arrive by FedEx or UPS truck, shipped to the pastor on installation day. It does not convey, along with the keys to the parsonage, as a new minister arrives to begin service to a small congregation in the rural South. Truly effective spiritual leadership takes time to emerge. It is formed by example, in relationship, as people get to know each other through meaningful connections in ministry and life.

Although not the primary focus of this book or even this chapter, it might be observed that many pastors today come and go from a congregation before, or without, earning much effective spiritual leadership. Their tenure is simply too short to enable and empower effective spiritual leadership of the community.

Can you be and become an effective spiritual leader in only twelve or eighteen months of pastoral ministry? Can you achieve this in two or three years? Possibly, if your gifts are exceptional, or if you are unusually transparent, or if you manifest spiritual gifts such as physical healing on a regular basis. A rare few might gain spiritual influence as a consequence of naturally charismatic personalities—this has been known to happen. But for most of us—men and women called into pastoral ministry—it takes years to develop effectiveness in spiritual leadership.

These years of leadership development are characterized by our mistakes and failures as well as our lucky decisions and apparent successes. Not all of our decisions are wise; not all of our judgments are sound. Some of our best ideas don't fit in our new context; some of our seminary classes are not useful in the real world, or at least not in the specific corner of the world in which we currently serve. So we adjust and learn, change and adapt, listen and discover—and over time people may decide that we are worthy of their trust, their empathy, and their respect.

Effective spiritual leadership is forged in service to a community of faith, developed as an outgrowth of personal character, observed over time. We are a mix of vices and virtues, strengths and weaknesses, wisdom and folly, and people know this and expect it. They allow us to lead when they decide that God is in us, that God can be trusted with us, and that we, as God's chosen shepherds, are honorable and sincere in our intentions. It also helps if we're humble.

The families in the pew expect their pastor to be their spiritual leader. The deacons around the conference table expect the same. If our discussion is merely about spiritual authority and spiritual leadership, there is a near-universal consensus that this real spiritual leadership is the domain of the pastor.

The challenge is how to translate an ethereal idea like "spiritual leadership" into daily decisions about what to do with a congregation's income, resources, or physical plant. When we start to talk about bricks and mortar, salaries and benefits, service times and worship styles, we have apparently moved away from "spiritual" matters and are now dealing with something else.

In these other matters, we may not expect (or even want) the pastor to be the leader or key decision maker. Instead, we may prefer to keep running the church the way it has always run—operating at the whim of an unelected church boss or under the influence of one or two key families who, after all, are "the main givers."

The Pastor Is Considered to Be an Employee of the Church

The apostle Paul traveled from city to city, planting churches. He drew his authority from his own call to ministry, plus the anointing of

God's Spirit through the hands of acknowledged Christian leaders. Although his own conversion was initially doubted (based on his previous track record of persecuting the church), Paul gained well-deserved influence as the impact of his ministry spread in the known world.

As he planted each new congregation, Paul was by no means an employee of the new entity. His aim was to locate and deploy local church leaders rather than to set up shop and become one. And even though he was entitled to compensation for his labors, Paul chose another route entirely. He supported his life and ministry by the work of his hands rather than by the offerings received in the plate.

Paul took up offerings, and Paul distributed those offerings—he just didn't make a living by drawing support from them personally. Paul provided his own way financially and then allocated church offerings to others around him. We may admire him for this wise practice; we may wish that we ourselves had this option. But for many of us, graduating from seminary after years of study and learning, our hope is that we can somehow obtain a paid role in ministry, preferably a role that will help us pare down our debt and pay off our massive student loans. We will probably not achieve these financial goals by selling our trinkets on eBay or by playing guitar on the streets. We are hoping (and praying) for gainful employment.

Generations of pastors have now gone forth to serve congregations with the expectation that they would be paid a salary to do so. Previous generations also had the expectation of a church-owned house in which to live; the current trend is to let the pastor establish credit and gain financial security by owning his own home.

Rare is the congregation or board that seeks, finds, and then pays for health insurance for the pastoral family; even rarer are communities of faith that locate and pay for such useful assistance as dental insurance or life insurance. Imagine a congregation paying for a policy that provides a large benefit to a pastor's spouse in the event of a sudden death. Have you ever heard of such a thing? Most likely not. The same goes for something as universally valuable as dental insurance.

Within the hallowed halls of seminaries, and on the sprawling campuses of today's Christian universities, you may hear some debate about the merits of a paid minister or of being paid to minister. These questions are theoretical in nature, and at times various responses may be passionately attacked or defended. But out where the campus ends and the real world begins, many aspiring pastors hope that their new congregation will pay them a decent salary, provide them with benefits, and perhaps help them a bit in their efforts to purchase a new home.

By seeking these financial benefits from the congregation, the pastor places himself or herself squarely in the role of an aspiring employee—a subservient role at best. So before we begin to complain about abuses of power or problems with the system as it now stands, perhaps we should at least admit that pastors like to be paid for their services. Fair enough?

Here is where the pastor's role becomes extremely ambiguous.

Message from the Misguided: We Own the Ranch

Remember Allen's story in the preface to this section?

Allen was interviewing for a pastoral role; the interview had gone fairly well. In a mostly social setting as the formal interview concluded, a church board member made the claim that "we [board, leaders] own the ranch, and we [key people] are going to hire ourselves a ranch hand."

Allen kept his outward composure but could hardly believe what he heard.

We own the ranch?

In Allen's theology, the church belongs to God, and its resources likewise belong to God—consecrated to God for his service, in his ministry. It would never occur to Allen that any group of people, anywhere, actually "owned the church" or felt that sense of entitlement or authority.

Allen came home from the interview in a state of shock and awe—negatively.

Yet Allen's experience is hardly unique. While the assumptions of a church board or congregation may not be stated so baldly or believed so blatantly, many do believe that the assets of the church belong to the church and that the financial resources of the church are *not* a matter where the pastor should lead.

After all, the pastor is merely an employee, right?

It is here, at the intersection of power and control, that pastors may find some of their most significant stress points in congregational ministry. While trying to lead (at least in spiritual matters) pastors are often being told to follow (with regard to financial, legal, and governance issues). These church policy and denominational polity issues are problematic, more so because few if any biblical models exist.

Jesus never led a church or pastored a congregation.

Paul planted churches but did not install himself as a permanent pastor to any of them. Meanwhile he supported himself by his own (secular) business.

In the Old Testament, the Levites served the ministry of the church and were supported by the tithes of the people. This is perhaps the clearest and most direct link to a paid ministry and/or paid staff. However, there is no indication from Scripture that the tithe-payers held any administrative and financial control over the tithe-receivers and their daily lives. Rather, it appears that the Levites administered their own resources as the tithes rolled in.

Hence the dilemma for modern believers: Who's in charge here?

Or to put it another way, the position of paid pastor comes pre-loaded with a high degree of role ambiguity—and thus the potential for large amounts of stress.

Case in Point No. 1: Darren's Dilemma

Fresh out of seminary, Darren answered the call of about forty faithful people in a rural setting far removed from where he was raised. Darren and his wife moved to the new community and were installed in an aging, repair-challenged parsonage.

Within a few weeks of arriving, Darren had his first meeting with the church board. His seminary course work had prepared him for exegetical study, sermon preparation, theological analysis, and much more. Nothing in seminary had told Darren how to lead or manage a church board.

As he attended that first meeting, Darren brought along a list of more than two dozen specific repair issues that needed to be addressed at the parsonage. He felt vaguely guilty for bringing these things up, yet at the same time he wondered how everyone in church had managed to miss these much-needed repairs. Had no one from the board even inspected the parsonage between pastors?

Darren, by his own description, was no handyman. His wife, who was as kind and flexible as anyone Darren knew, had been pretty good-natured about moving into a house that needed such basic attention. As he prepared for that first meeting with the board, Darren made a bullet-point presentation about what he regarded as the top five issues in the parsonage—those needing an immediate response.

Here are Darren's five bullet points from that meeting:

- The front door will not lock; the lock itself is broken. It is impossible to lock and secure the parsonage whenever we are gone.
- The kitchen sink leaks every time we put water in it. There appears to be a seal missing, or a very cracked and broken seal

at best. If we run water in the kitchen sink—any time, every time—it leaks down into the cabinet below and out onto the kitchen floor.

- The heating elements in the oven do not work. They do not turn red or get hot or give any sign of heating anything. This may be as simple as a fuse (?) or something easy to fix. But no matter what we do, we are not able to get any heat in the oven. So, the oven does not work.

- Four window screens are badly torn; the tears are too large to tape over or seal in some other way. Since we so often have the windows open for outside air, we really need screens. I am glad to install these myself; I think this repair is something I can do, if the church buys some new screens for these four windows. (Two other windows have small tears in the screens but we can live with those.)

- The floor in the bathroom appears to be rotted. The floor sags and feels like you might fall right through it. There is linoleum on the floor, so we have not pulled it up to check on this, but it makes us nervous.

Try to remember: Darren and his wife had identified about two dozen of these repair projects. Darren only made bullet points out of his "top five" issues. Although he felt guilty about being the one to bring up these things, Darren also felt a sense of duty to his young wife. He wanted her to be happy in her new home, since both of them had moved far away from family and friends. And since the church owned the parsonage, Darren believed that the church board members would feel responsible for keeping their pastor's house in good repair and in good working order.

Darren was about to be disappointed.

"For the next two years, I kept bringing issues to the attention of the board." Darren sighs. "I didn't bring this up at every meeting. I would wait a month or two, and then bring the top four or five issues. But out of all that time, we had maybe three things fixed while we lived there. And those three were kind of random. It was almost like the things that got fixed were whatever the guys in the church wanted to work on personally. If the project didn't interest the two or three guys who ran the church—if they didn't want to work on it themselves—nothing ever got done."

Darren pauses before resuming his narrative.

"Almost nothing got fixed or replaced," he says quietly. "The few projects they did tackle took forever to complete. The guys would wander in and out of our house like they lived there themselves. One of them didn't even knock when he came over. And since the front door didn't have a working lock, he could just walk right in.

"Would you live that way?" Darren asks us as we interview him. "Would you put up with that for two years? In two years' time, we never had a front door that would lock. Okay, we were in a small town, and maybe people have different values, and they trust their neighbors or whatever. But is it unreasonable to want to lock your door when you leave for a few hours? And what about Sunday mornings? Everyone knew we wouldn't be home on Sunday mornings. Anyone and everyone could have walked right in, toured our home, and walked out the front door with whatever they wanted to take."

Darren shakes his head, remembering.

"I had no control over such a basic, fundamental part of church life," he tells us at a busy Bob Evans restaurant. "Every meeting was like a subtle reminder that I didn't have any power over the finances or the priorities. I was supposed to be the preacher and visit the sick people, but I didn't have a voice in decisions about what to do with our money or whether or not to repair the parsonage.

"I felt totally powerless in the situation," he admits. "I felt like I was not the leader of these people. Every time they ignored a simple repair or refused to finance something easy, like new screens for our windows, I felt like my leadership was being rejected. I felt like a newly hired employee with no seniority, no importance, and definitely no voice.

"That's not the only reason we left," Darren allows as our conversation continues. "There were some other things going on in the church too. But after about a year of struggling with that, I started talking to a few DSs I had met while I was in seminary. I asked them about opportunities on their districts. I would call them or e-mail them and just ask about any openings.

"One of those DSs had become a friend during his visits to seminary, and I trusted him to be honest with me about how things really were. One day I called him and told him about our top ten repair issues in the parsonage, and I just kind of vented and complained and whined to him for a while. And he wasn't even the DS of my district! But I felt a lot better, although I worried that maybe I had just ruined a good friendship with this guy."

Darren gives us a wry grin.

"Exactly the opposite happened," he says with a smile. "That DS called me about eight months later with an opportunity on his district. The church was about the same size as mine, and it was raising about the same amount of money as we were. So there was no sense of a promotion or upward career move or anything. But the first thing that DS said on the phone was 'Darren, you've got to see the parsonage over here. It is only three years old and it is absolutely beautiful!'"

The young pastor nods his head slowly.

"Before you start judging me, just put yourself in my place," he suggests. "You're new at being married, you're new at being a pastor, and you are living in this run-down, old house that no one wants to fix up. And you're out there visiting and calling and taking care of people, just hoping someone will repair your oven or buy you some inexpensive screens. But it never happens, no matter how often you ask or how often you bring it up at a board meeting.

"Then you get a phone call, and by saying 'yes,' you can move into an almost-new house and be employed by a church that cares about the condition of its pastor's home. Now, honestly, I know we are all supposed to be spiritual and sanctified and whatever, but if you were in my place, what would you do?"

The question is mostly rhetorical.

Darren and his wife went to visit the prospective new church. The DS met them a few miles outside of town and drove them to the parsonage first before also showing them the church building. Since the previous pastor was already gone, the parsonage was empty and ready for their inspection.

"My wife cried," Darren recalls. "She cried while we were walking through it. And we hadn't even told the DS that he could put our name in for that position. We had just gone over there to take a look around and then talk to the superintendent. But my wife walked into that kitchen and saw how fresh and nice everything was, and she just broke down and started crying."

Darren pauses and looks directly at us.

"Judge me if you will," he says firmly. "But right then and there, I decided that we were moving and that my wife was going to live in that house. If that's not holy, then so be it. But I was tired of it and she was tired of it and here was a way to work just as hard as I already was, and get paid about the same as I already was, but live in a nice, clean, almost-new house that was in great repair.

"I told the DS he could put my name in. I told him if the congregation voted for us we'd be there, no questions asked. And after that, it seemed like it all happened pretty fast."

Darren and his wife accepted the new call, said their good-byes to their first-ever congregation, packed up a moving truck, and moved away from a run-down, ramshackle house that was nearly eighty years old and looked older. They drove a few states away and unpacked into an almost-new parsonage. On the day they arrived, the

DS and his wife were waiting in the driveway; the superintendent's wife had brought along a fresh-baked pie and a half-gallon of vanilla ice cream in a cooler.

"This is for you," the DSs wife said to Darren's wife. "Welcome to your new home, and we hope you live here for a long time."

With that friendly greeting, the two couples unlocked the parsonage (it had a front door with a working lock!), went inside, and stood around the empty kitchen eating pie and ice cream on paper plates, using plastic forks.

"That pie was the best thing I ever tasted," Darren remembers.

If you do not serve in pastoral ministry, are you surprised that a pastoral move might come down to such a simple equation: Newer house versus never-repaired old house? If you do serve in pastoral ministry, do you have similar stories you can tell from your own experience?

Darren and his wife made their choice and never regretted it.

"They had me at the kitchen," is how Darren summarizes his process.

Case in Point No. 2: Michael's Mistake

Michael planted a church, answering an ad in his seminary newspaper.

After interviewing with the superintendent, Michael was screened by a process that helps identify personality traits, temperament issues, and the general suitability of church planting for prospective pastors.

"We passed all our assessments," Michael remembers. "And we were so excited about planting a new church. The district had a core group of people ready, gathered from several other churches nearby. Many of the core group families were committed to staying with us; a few were volunteering to help us get started, with the understanding that later they would return to their home churches."

Michael and his wife began the adventure of a lifetime.

"We set up an office very cheaply," he tells us, "and we started renting another church on Sunday evenings. It was an unconventional start—most churches begin with Sunday morning services—but it worked for us. We saw God bring us quite a few families in those first six or eight months, even though we were having church at 6 P.M. on Sunday. We'd gather for a fellowship meal about 5 P.M., which was just low-key and all about making connections, then we'd have church at 6 P.M. and be done and home by about 8. It was unusual, but it worked pretty well."

The church grew in attendance and began raising enough funds to cover the rent on the church, plus pay the pastor a small salary. Meanwhile the district was committed to pay the pastor's salary in full for the first year, then at half-rate for the second year. After that, the church was on its own financially.

Looking back, Michael wishes he had handled one area differently.

"My wife is a trained accountant," Michael tells us. "She was a business major with an accounting minor, and she had worked in accounting for two different companies. Both of them gave her raises and good reviews.

"So when we planted the new church, I asked her to run the finances. She didn't want to—I wish I had listened to her—but I kind of guilted her into doing it. She had the background and the training and the skills, plus obviously I trusted her completely. It's not like we were raising huge sums of money back then, especially at the start, but she could have done the books for a megachurch. She's that good."

Reluctantly, Michael's wife began serving as the treasurer of the church, handling everything from offerings and collections to accounts payable and payroll.

"She asked me several times if she could quit doing that," Michael says, "and I should have listened to her. Instead I just told her what a great job she was doing, and I kind of made her keep doing it."

All went well for the first year and a half.

Then the church was growing and expanding and raising more money. The pastor quit taking district support—early—because the church could afford to fully cover his salary, rental costs, and other expenses like advertising and mailing. The church began renting a billboard on the outskirts of town, telling people where to find the new church, and about the unusual, Sunday-evening time for services.

"I hear all these stories about church plants not working out," Michael tells us, "but we had the opposite problem. We were succeeding, and we were especially doing well financially. We were attracting families that already knew how to tithe and had already learned how to be faithful. Many of them had church backgrounds and had served on church boards. At the time I was elated about that. Now as I look back, I can see how we got in trouble."

About two years into the church planting process, Michael realized that the wives of key church leaders were openly critical of his wife. She was not making friends among the women of the church; a few of them openly shunned her. Michael worried about it but was busy taking care of many other things. He reasoned that perhaps other women were jealous of his wife for being married to the pastor. He wondered if perhaps they were jealous of her appearance: she was beautiful.

Yet the problematic issue was elsewhere, in an undercurrent of unease.

Behind Michael's back, key church leaders were asking questions like these:

"Why is the pastor's wife handling all the money around here?"

"Why is the pastor's wife the one who keeps the church checkbook?"

"Why is the pastor's wife in charge of the people who count the offering?"

"How long are we going to put up with this?"

Church leaders were restless and active, but they didn't bring their concerns directly to Michael. Instead, gossip and rumors began flowing freely, and before long half the church was convinced that Michael's wife was skimming money off the top of the church offerings. After all, wasn't she always wearing new clothes? After all, weren't those designer handbags she was carrying? How could she afford to dress like that? There was only one conclusion: she must be stealing from the offerings.

As the rumors flew, Michael's wife tried repeatedly to make friends, to have coffee with other wives, and to help assimilate new members into the fellowship. Yet no matter how hard she tried, Michael's wife remembers feeling like an outsider, someone who just couldn't break in to the inner circle.

"And we had planted this church!" Michael reminds us. "This is not like we moved to a church that was established, and all the social circles were already in place. My wife was going crazy wondering why nobody liked her, nobody would return her phone calls, and nobody would invite her or include her in things."

Michael shakes his head.

"I was an idiot," he says with disgust. "I mean, our finances were in great shape and Melissa was doing excellent work with the accounting. But once the rumors broke out in the open, it was already too late to repair the damage. No matter what the truth was, everyone believed that my wife had been stealing from the offerings and was living large on church funds."

When the rumors finally reached the surface, Michael commissioned a full church audit by an outside accounting firm. The audit results weren't returned for about three months, but came back affirming the accuracy and clarity of the work Michael's wife had been doing.

"She was completely vindicated by the auditors," Michael says in an animated voice, his volume growing louder. "They actually complimented her for what an excellent job she had done! But by then, it no longer mattered. People had already made up their minds. They had already judged her and found her guilty. No matter what the auditors said, people kept believing my wife was a thief."

Although he had planted the church from nothing, and although the church was growing and succeeding in every category, Michael began making strategic phone calls to other places, looking for a way to leave. Almost immediately he was offered a larger church a long distance from the church plant. There would be a higher salary and a better life, but Michael's only reason for leaving was that his wife was being shamed and rejected by the women in their current church.

"That's the only reason we left, but it was a big deal," Michael sighs. "I mean, things were going really well. Everyone could see that. But I wasn't willing to make my wife stay there and keep on being an outsider. Even after the auditors came back with their praise and compliments, nothing changed. Everyone still believed what they wanted to believe. My wife was afraid to wear new shoes or carry a new purse or show up in a new dress or new slacks. She started being really self-conscious about her wardrobe and her jewelry and her hair.

"Let's face it: some things are just not worth the trouble," Michael opines as he sags backward into his chair. "Why put someone through all that? It was so totally unfair to her. Also I believed it was mostly my fault anyway—I was the one who kind of forced her into doing all of the accounting and financial stuff."

Michael and his wife answered the call, abandoned the church they planted, and moved several states away to a larger assignment. There, despite her obvious gifts in accounting and finance, Michael made sure his wife had nothing to do with the offerings, the counting, the reporting, or the accounts payable.

"She made friends right away," Michael says of the new setting. "She's a beautiful person—she's a lot nicer than I am, and everybody loves her immediately. So looking back, I'm really glad we moved, but I'm also mad at myself for putting her in that very uncomfortable situation. And I'm totally convinced that if we went back [to the church plant], everyone would still look at her like she was a thief.

"Isn't that bizarre?" Michael asks us without wanting an answer. "People are so ready to judge, so ready to leap to the wrong conclusion. Anyway, we're beyond that now and my wife has a ton of friends in our new church. I love watching her lead the women here and be respected by the women here. It's such good therapy for me to see that happening."

By trying to take authority over financial issues—a move made easier by the fact that he was the founding pastor and the planter of the church—Michael ended up in relational and political trouble. His wife was disrespected by people who quietly believed she was stealing from church funds. Michael's ministry might have continued for a while, but his choice was flight, not fight—in essence the same choice that Darren also made, but for different reasons.

While Darren fled because he couldn't achieve effective control over financial issues, Michael took flight because his efforts to establish and maintain control ultimately led to unexpected consequences. Both pastors were responding to role ambiguity as it impacts the financial administration of the congregation. Both made the choice of flight, instead of fighting. It is not always so.

We ask Darren if he would make these same choices again. "Absolutely," Darren tells us. "No regrets at all. My wife and I are enjoying our best days in ministry here—in ways that would never have been possible at [prior setting]."

We ask Michael if he would make these same choices again.

"No way," Michael replies quickly. "I'd rather live with terrible accounting and sloppy reporting and everything else that goes with it. I could put up with that stuff a lot more easily than watching my wife be rejected and disrespected. I wish I hadn't kept control of the finances, and I wish I hadn't put my wife through all that.

"But regardless," Michael says hurriedly, "that's all behind us now. In our new church, everyone loves my wife and things are going great!"

Approaches Toward Addressing Role Ambiguity

This is a book about helping pastors cope with stressful situations. It is not, per se, a book about church governance. Having said that, here are two of the many ways in which questions of role ambiguity have been addressed by church structure or church policy, with varying degrees of success.

Plant the Church, Plant the Leaders

Some denominations and groups have borrowed a model from independent churches with regard to planting new congregations. In this model, the planter has a wide degree of latitude in setting up leadership and control of the new entity.

In some settings, the church planter will be tasked with locating, identifying, and then training his or her church board and group of spiritual leaders. Rather than reporting to a preexisting panel of controlling interests and conflicting opinions, the pastor/planter personally selects those who will comprise the board of governance. In this way, the church planter exercises a great deal of authority over what types of temperaments and gifts, attitudes and views will populate the governing body.

From a distance, especially from the perspective of a pastor facing off against a troubled or hostile church board, this approach seems highly attractive. What minister would turn down the opportunity to hand-select his or her leadership team? What pastor wouldn't want to have the ultimate and final power over determining who serves on the board, and who doesn't serve on the board? Even the gentlest of pastoral personalities might find this opportunity simply too appealing to resist.

The drawbacks of this approach are evident in advance. An insecure leader may surround himself or herself with only those who share his or her own perspective and biases. An overly controlling pastor may preselect a church board whose members are relatively pliant, assuring that the force of his or her own personality will win the day.

Those who oppose this practice remind us that power corrupts, and absolute power corrupts absolutely. They believe that a pastor-selected board is a recipe for disaster—later, if not sooner. They believe that this model gives far too much power and authority to the pastor or leader.

To date, the "plant the church, plant the leaders" model exists in varying quantities and in diverse places but has not gained widespread acceptance as a replacement for more traditional patterns of authority and governance. This leaves local church boards with a great deal of power and authority over the business matters of the church, including the disposition of its financial assets.

The Staff-Led Versus Board-Led Church

Another model of resolving role ambiguity is suggested by the process of having a staff-led church. In this model, although there is a church board drawn from the laity of the congregation, this board serves mostly in an advisory role, at the request of the senior pastor. The pastor may heed or ignore any advice he or she receives from this group, since their role is primarily to consult or recommend.

In this model, the church staff is essentially in governance or leadership of the direction, priorities, and processes of the congregation. The senior pastor hires church staff and gives them a wide range of latitude in achieving the mission and reaching the goals of the church body. Freed from functional oversight by the church board, the staff can often decide how to allocate resources, how to plan for the current fiscal year and future budgets, and what decisions to make en route.

Examples of staff-led churches occur more often in independent churches or in larger or megachurches that are affiliated with denominations. To some extent, even a well-established denomination is unlikely to "mess with success." If a local body of believers is growing and flourishing under a staff-led model, denominational leaders are much less likely to intervene or to complain about governance issues.

As in "plant the leaders," this model effectively relieves the local church board of most of its usual or typical powers and responsibilities. Instead of making the key decisions and then supervising the pastor and staff, the church board in this model is somewhat passive and disengaged from these issues. The board may be drawn in, usually at the request of the senior pastor, to give advice or counsel about major issues like selling a property, entering a new phase of a building campaign, or other similar priorities. Yet on a day-to-day basis, the staff (not the board) plans and directs the business and administrative life of the church.

The staff-led model resolves much or most of the role ambiguity that is extant in pastoral settings. In this model, issues of power and control are clearly under the authority of the lead pastor and the staff, with advisory input from a lay board. In the view of some, this simplifies the decision-making process and frees up the pastor to minister and lead, without worrying about catering to egos and biases among the laity. This approach appears to have a high view of clergy and a lower view of laity.

Pastoral Temperaments and Responses

The degree or extent to which role ambiguity functions as a stressor is impacted by the personality and temperament of the pastor. In a later chapter, we will establish a framework for responding to stress and learning to thrive. As we conclude our look at role ambiguity, we will take a quick look at how temperament and personality can interact with ambiguity and leadership issues.

A pastor with a high interest in control may attempt to address ambiguity by establishing himself or herself as the undisputed leader of the congregation. This leadership is not limited to merely spiritual matters but also extends to temporal issues and the de facto governance of the larger group. Think of this pastoral type as a dictator or manipulator, benevolent or otherwise.

Sit down with long-established lay members of a congregation and ask them to review their history of pastors, and it's not unusual for at least one minister of this type to occur within the church's history. While we may think of a power-driven or dictatorial temperament as being a negative characteristic, it is not always regarded this way by those who experience it.

Pastors who lead with a high level of central authority and control can and do produce positive results or engender positive responses. If the worship services are well-ordered or if significant progress is made in raising money or building new facilities, a dictator/pastor may be highly regarded in the present moment and also through the longer lens of church history. So at least to some extent, reaction to a dictatorial temperament may vary depending on the amount of apparent "success" the pastor had, using the common metrics of church life: attendance, finances, expansion or remodeling of the building, and so on.

The dictatorial pastor may not be troubled by role ambiguity but may instead frame the problem as a matter of "getting everyone to hear from God" or "getting us all on the same page." Either of these expressions, sincerely used, may actually refer to a process by which the pastor gains, holds, and extends personal authority or the decisions of the larger body.

Another common pastoral temperament is the people-pleasing type. In the case of a people-pleaser, the traumas of role ambiguity may be minimized by the fact that the pastor aims to please or gain the respect of key lay leaders. This pastoral type will flatter, acquiesce, agree, or defer as a way of moving forward. The result may be a high degree of perceived unity in the leadership, which exists primarily because the pastor sublimates or sets aside his or her own priorities.

Surprisingly, the people-pleasing pastor is not always highly regarded. In the case of a local congregation being controlled by a few key persons or main families, there may be a disenfranchised group among the laity who wish that their pastor would finally "stand up to Bill" or "get the Joneses off the board." While the pastor is busy pleasing the powers that be, others are wishing those powers would cease. The result can be a short-term apparent success for church life, but a longer-term stalemate or even a disaster. Issues of power and control are quickly divisive and can be long-lived. Over time, the disenfranchised and voiceless tend to migrate to other flocks, leaving power even more centralized among key lay leaders.

Each of these ways of responding to ambiguity—taking control decisively or relinquishing control too easily—is often simpler than the difficult give-and-take of adjusting to a situation that is ambiguous by polity and definition. To some extent, the current iteration of much church governance is impacted by the same mind-set that established three branches of governance for the United States of America: legislative, judicial, and executive. For better or worse, the USA's founding fathers hoped to avoid centralizing too much power in any one branch. Instead, they envisioned a nation with checks and balances in place, so that no one person or institution could gain or exert undue influence.

Typical church governance displays a similar mind-set, tacitly or explicitly. Declining to give absolute power to the pastor, yet insisting that the pastor be the "spiritual leader" of the congregation, appears to set up a checks-and-balances mind-set. In many ways, the current church model draws from political experiences in the

Western world, particularly recent Western democracies such as the United States.

Until things change, a typical context looks like this: the pastor will have one area of authority (spiritual); the church board another (material). Whether this model and method results in a healthy balance of power or an unhealthy degree of ambiguity can be debated for years to come. Meanwhile, those who serve in this model as pastoral leaders will continue to deal with an ambiguity of role that causes short-term or longer-term stress. Among pastors of various denominations and in diverse cultures, role ambiguity is often the first stressor cited, or is the stressor ranked highest in importance or level of difficulty.

The role of pastor in the early twenty-first century is indeed ambiguous.

4
SIGNIFICANT STRESSOR: PERFORMANCE ANXIETY

Calvin has a wry sense of humor.

Nearly three years into a troubled pastorate, Calvin has agreed to meet us for coffee as we research and write this new book. We're in a family restaurant that is several towns away from the place of Calvin's ministry. While his family shops at a nearby Walmart, we are interviewing Calvin about his pastoral experience.

"Things were bad when I got here," Calvin says with a perfectly timed comedic pause, "but I am gradually making things worse."

He grins at us, and then looks at his shoes.

We recognize and appreciate both the humor of Calvin's remark—he is a genuinely funny guy—and also the underlying notes of sorrow and perhaps regret. We'll learn, as we sip coffee and listen carefully, that Calvin's self-esteem and his sense of self-worth have been steadily plummeting since he arrived to serve this waning congregation. After a less than stellar start at his first church, Calvin moved across the country to accept this call, his second assignment in pastoral ministry.

"I've given this my best shot, but now I am just about worn out." Calvin sighs. "My family is worn out. We have invested all our prayers and all our hopes and all our energies into this place, and it seems like no matter what I do, no matter what I might try, things just keep going downhill."

Calvin pauses for a moment.

"When I arrived here and kind of sized things up, I decided that much of the blame for the previous decline could be traced to the previous pastor. Maybe that's not fair to him, but that was my read on it. I looked at the charts and talked to some of the pastors in the area and everything pointed to my predecessor as being the problem. He was about to retire when he came here, and then frankly he stayed too long and delayed his retirement in a way that hurt the church.

"He was four or five years away from retiring when he took this church, and he told folks he would only stay for four or five years. He was very open about that. But then he ended up staying for eleven years. Eleven years! And it's not a problem that he was older—I have no issue with that—the problem is he just didn't invest much energy or intensity into this setting, not even when he began his ministry here. He came here to retire; that was his mind-set from the beginning. Then he pastored here with that mind-set for more than a decade.

"How do you think that affects a church, when the pastor is just kind of marking time until his retirement? How do you think it affects a church when that same pastor hangs around for eleven years, mostly just marking time? I mean, I want to be fair to the guy, I really do. But he came here openly telling folks that he was four or five years from retiring. He wanted to serve here, and then be done.

"But instead of retiring when he said he would, he just kept drawing a salary and doing the same old things over and over. He was gentle and friendly, but he ended up presiding over a slow but steady decline in the key membership numbers. The older people died off, and he preached their funerals. The younger people drifted away, and he didn't chase after them. There weren't any young families attending. There wasn't a youth group—at all. And I knew all that before I arrived."

Calvin sighs again.

"I came here believing that I understood the dynamics here, and I understood the problems here, and really thinking that I was the right guy to turn things around. Does that sound proud or conceited to you? I don't mean it that way."

Calvin pauses to study our expressions, which are neutral. Sensing no judgment or condemnation from us (and we felt none), he resumes his narrative.

"Honestly, I believed I could turn this place around," the pastor continues. "My kids were a few years away from being in a youth group. I thought that I could develop a youth group by the time they got to that age. I knew I could attract and keep some younger families, people the same age as my wife and I. I felt like we could draw and attract some couples like us, and they'd have kids, and that way we'd build a nucleus that would end up building the church.

"I mean, I had this all figured out. I knew what the problems had been, and I knew I was the answer to them. Not that I'm some hot-shot preacher or God's gift to pastoral ministry—I'm not! I know that. But I'm a good guy, and I preach okay, and after all, didn't God call me here? I thought we'd be fine."

Calvin pauses.

"I believe God did that—I believe God called me. So right along with that, my belief was that God was ready to turn this place around. I believed that God had chosen me as his person, his pastor, to reverse the years of decline here."

There is a brief gap as Calvin sips coffee and looks thoughtful. We wait, knowing from long experience that sometimes wisdom needs time to percolate.

We sense the shadows of self-doubt when Calvin resumes speaking.

"I still believe God called me here," Calvin says slowly. "But I'm not sure anymore that I'm capable of effective ministry. I guess that's the bottom line, at least for me personally. I believe in God, I believe in his call, but I am steadily losing faith in the guy in the mirror: me. I am really starting to wonder if I've got what it takes. And if I don't—I don't want to end up as that old guy who doesn't know when to retire, the out-of-touch guy who doesn't know how to gracefully find the exit."

Calvin stops to make eye contact with us.

"Does any of this make sense?" he asks, mostly rhetorically.

The Choices behind the Circumstances

For the next forty-five minutes as we sit together in a popular family restaurant during their midafternoon lull, we'll ask Calvin some questions about the context rather than about his personal experience. We will deliberately change the subject, allowing Calvin to talk about the history of the church since he arrived, including major decisions and the events that have shaped this community of faith during his pastorate. We're hoping to find some clues in the context that will help us understand the downward trajectory of the metrics in this place.

Calvin's church was in gradual decline for eleven years before he arrived. His church has remained in gradual decline since he arrived three years ago. This overarching trend is quite visible from a distance, as well as up close. Still, as Calvin connects the dots, he ends up blaming himself for the current state of the church. Calvin believes that his own failures and shortcomings have contributed to the gradual loss of attendance and financial support during the past three years. He's not noticing the fourteen-year pattern; he's locked into looking at only three of these past fourteen years. So if we're going to help this young pastor correctly view the broader picture, we need to know about the choices and decisions the church has made during Calvin's brief tenure in this place. We ask him about that.

"The first thing I tried to do was make our worship more contemporary," Calvin says with evident enthusiasm. "And I really shouldn't even use the word *contemporary* when I talk about it. Actually, I tried to get the church to go from a very traditional worship style to something you might call blended. I don't like the term *blended,* and I personally like worship that is all the way contemporary—I like to rock out in worship—but I didn't try to take this church to that level.

"All I wanted to do was make our worship a bit more appealing," Calvin says. "I hoped that our preaching had just gotten an upgrade—forgive me for sounding so prideful—and I thought that we should upgrade our worship the same way. We had a young single guy in our congregation—he was a science teacher at the local high school—and I asked him to play guitar for some of the songs we sang.

"Now, this guy was not personally very dynamic, and we didn't need him to be that way. He was actually a nerdy science teacher type. But he played guitar well, and just having the guitar accompany the songs was a nice change from what the church had been doing—or that's how it seemed to me.

"When we sang some of the newer choruses, instead of using the hymnal, sometimes the guitar would be the only accompaniment. There was nothing like rock music happening—we had a nerdy science teacher playing an acoustic guitar while accompanying us on very well-known choruses. It was Gaither stuff. Classic choruses from the eighties and nineties. That's what I tried to put in our worship mix."

Calvin looks at his hands.

"We tried that for maybe two months," he recounts. "And I thought it was going pretty well. My kids were enjoying it. They still weren't teens, but they were getting closer to that time in their lives. I think my kids enjoyed seeing the guitar on the stage, and I think they were able to worship better because of that.

"Anyway," Calvin says, sighing, "my experiment with the guitar didn't get very far. After only a month or two, one of the main elders asked if he could meet with me. When I sat down to meet with him, he told me that the board wanted me to know that it wasn't okay to have drums on the platform.

"Just so you understand—we had never tried drums on the platform, and there wasn't a drummer in the church, and I had no plans for drums in the future," Calvin says, shaking his head.

"Just so you realize—we had been using an acoustic guitar only. No drums or tambourines, nobody dancing around on the platform, nobody rocking out. We just had a science teacher and his lone guitar."

Calvin wrinkles his face into a wry smile.

"I wasn't pushing the envelope, I was barely even nudging it," he says with a slight grin. "We weren't 'out there' in worship, and we weren't heading out there. . . ."

Even so, the church board apparently feared for the future of the church.

"That particular elder told me that the whole church board was worried about the direction of our church, and worried that I might try to put drums on the platform. He told me that several other churches in town had put drums on their platforms, and that those churches had gone to the devil. Those were his actual words— those churches had gone to the devil. So apparently, at least in the minds of some on my board, the devil is in the drums. Who knew?"

Having been drawn into far too many conversations about worship styles, in far too many places, we pass on the chance to discuss how worship should be done or ought to be done or might be done. We glance at each other, resolving never to write a book about worship styles—or at least not a book of our recommendations.

Since we don't engage with him on this hot topic, Calvin moves on to the next major event in the church's progression since his arrival.

"After that I started using the science teacher less and less," Calvin says softly. "I didn't talk to him about it. I didn't tell him that a board member had come to me or anything. I didn't want him to take it personally.

"I just kind of phased down our use of the guitar. I would have him play his guitar maybe once a month or so, and usually on Sunday nights. A lot of my good board members missed our Sunday night services, even though they insisted that we keep having them. So while my board members were home watching football on TV, every once in a while I would have the guy play his guitar for Sunday night. Otherwise I gave up on trying to get us to move forward in the way we did worship."

Calvin is quiet before continuing.

"The next idea I came up with was maybe selling our building," he continues. "We actually own two buildings—a smaller one that was once the original church, and a larger building that is now mostly sanctuary, which was added in the 1970s. The original church building got converted to classrooms and office space, while the 'new' addition was built to be a sanctuary, two restrooms, and one small office.

"We have two buildings, one of which is a sanctuary that can seat at least three hundred people, probably more," Calvin tells us. "Back in the day, we had been one of the larger churches in our small town for a while, maybe twenty or thirty years ago. But gradually the crowd had been declining and we were getting together as maybe only forty people, forty-five people, sometimes up to sixty people on Easter Sunday—in a space that could seat three hundred or more.

"It was depressing, at least to me," Calvin admits. "So after thinking about it for a while, I talked to the board about putting our church buildings on the market and perhaps trying to meet in the high school cafeteria for a while. We had an almost-new high school in town with great facilities. The auditorium was amazing—it would seat even more people than our sanctuary. So we didn't need to use the auditorium, but the high school cafeteria was just the right size for us. We could set up over in one corner of the space, roll a piano down the hall from the music room, and share worship together, followed by a fellowship meal.

"The night I presented that idea to the board was the quietest board meeting we've had in three years," Calvin remembers. "Nobody said anything at all. My dreams and ideas—and they were only ideas, after all, I hadn't taken any action—just kind of hung out there in space, with nobody breathing. Nobody opposed the ideas, at least not out loud, but nobody supported them either.

"I talked all the way through the possibilities, looked around the room, reviewed everything again to sum up some of the potential positives. And then the room was silent. When I didn't get any responses, I finally asked people what they thought about it. And even after that, nobody made any effort to respond.

"We pressed ahead to some other agenda items and we had a very routine board meeting, trying to decide whether or not to spend twenty-five dollars on something or other. When we finally finished with the last item, the secretary asked the treasurer to pray as we closed the meeting. And then the treasurer prayed this very long prayer, thanking God for the way he had faithfully led us along, and thanking God especially for the beautiful church building that we all enjoyed."

Calvin is silent.

"So basically, after trying and failing to update our worship styles, the next brilliant idea I suggested was that we barbecue our sacred cow. . . ."

Calvin's gift for ironic wordplay is amusing, and we smile appropriately.

He notices our response and seems to be grateful.

"You understand, I was just talking about an idea here," he tells us with mild amazement. "I wasn't making a motion. I hadn't talked to a Realtor about this. I didn't even know if the high school would let us use their cafeteria or how much it would cost. I was just kind of brainstorming ideas—and all I got was dead silence and then this prayer that kind of put me in my place, thanking God for the building. . . ."

Calvin is silent.

"I guess I always thought I was a natural leader," he says slowly. "I mean, I didn't think I was somebody like Bill Hybels or Rick Warren—I just thought I had some leadership qualities that made people follow me, at least a little bit.

"After that meeting, I started wondering if I was wrong about my gifts of leadership or wrong about my call to ministry or wrong about hearing God call us to serve in that place.

"I'm not sure exactly how I felt at that moment, but I can tell you that I didn't feel like a success. I didn't feel like a good leader. I didn't feel like anyone respected or valued my ideas about how to grow our church. In fact, I felt just the opposite. . . ."

Calvin's voice trails off just as his family arrives, with Walmart bags in hand. We smile at the children, Lisa greets Calvin's wife, and our interview hits the "pause" button for a while. We order dessert for the whole family, and we sit for a while, laughing and talking and getting acquainted. As a husband and a father, Calvin appears to be a roaring success—and we are delighted to watch as he is respected and valued by his wife and children. Calvin is succeeding in the arena that is closest to our hearts—his family circle.

The Evaporation of Self-Esteem

Calvin's story, to which we'll return later, typifies the experiences of many pastors who minister in difficult or challenging settings. Whether serving their first or their fourth pastorate, these gifted servants of God find themselves troubled by the direction of many relevant metrics, such as attendance, giving, new members, or professions of faith. Without considering the denominational or up-line expectations (which deserve a separate book of their own), these pastors are afflicted with varying degrees of self-doubt or anxiety about their own performances. They may draw the conclusion, as Calvin does in our interview, that their gifts and graces are not a good fit for pastoral ministry.

Across divisions of age and race, gender and zip code, denomination and setting, pastors worry about whether or not they are "getting the job done" or "making a go of it" in their current situations. It is a particularly male characteristic to draw self-esteem from the workplace and from the career, and it is also a marker for pastors and those who serve in ministry. Too often, our sense of worth and value depends on how things seem to be going in the moment.

For the few who are lucky or gifted, relevant markers may indicate an upturn. The congregation is growing, the people are giving more generously than before, new believers are being baptized. There is a positive momentum in these events, which tends to generate positive self-esteem among the ministers who experience them. While it is true that not all success can be traced to a pastor or person, and that not all growth is actually success, it is also true that a rising tide lifts all boats. The pastor who presides over growth and financial progress tends to feel better about his or her ministry and gifts.

By contrast, the pastor who serves in a time of stasis or slow decline may eventually conclude that these markers in the external environment are indicators of deficiencies in his or her gifts, character, or training. While a tough and durable sense of personal identity and gifting can survive one negative pastoral setting or perhaps two settings in which little or no growth occurs, sooner or later the realities of declining metrics tend to produce self-doubt and anxiety in the minister. Few of us are so naturally confident that we can ignore what seems to be happening in the offering plate or the attendance numbers.

When things are going well, we feel great about ourselves.

When things seem to be going downhill, our anxiety is tangible.

Larry, who is serving his third pastorate just as his wife prepares to deliver their first baby, is notably sanguine about this trend. "If I can't make things work this time, I think I'll just leave the ministry and try something else," Larry tells us at a busy and popular conference for pastors. "This is my third try, so I guess if I whiff this one, it's my third strike. So I'm out. . . ."

Larry goes on to tell us about his first two pastoral settings, one of which ended in unresolved conflict. The other situation ended because after almost four years of serving, Larry realized that he wasn't seeing growth. He didn't believe he was making a difference or bringing positive change. So he called a few friends, mentioned that he was looking for a new position, and received an offer within a matter of only a few months. He jumped at the chance for a new beginning.

"Somebody is always desperate, somewhere," is how Larry describes his ability to find a new place to serve. Despite his use of self-deprecating humor, Larry articulates a reality among some denominations and places. Given the small size of many congregations and the relatively low budgets they have available, a growing number of churches may be unable to attract and hold talented ministers.

"With the salary I can offer at most of my smaller churches," one longer-term DS tells us, "I'm lucky when anyone returns my calls. The truth is that many of my guys [gender reference that of the speaker] are bivocational, and a lot more of them will be bivocational soon. Our churches just don't pay enough to make it possible for a pastor to earn a decent living. So it seems like I've always got a church to fill, and it seems like I'm always making about half an offer, in terms of the financial package I can present to a prospect."

Others in leadership tell us similar stories. We'll devote our next chapter to the challenges faced by bivocational pastors, but for the purposes of this current discussion, what matters is that smaller churches are unable to seek and find the type of candidates they might prefer. They aren't offering enough pay, don't have enough bodies in the pews, and don't appear to be prospective environments for future growth and success, as measured in human terms.

All of this adds substance to Larry's witty remark about someone always being desperate. There's a ring of self-doubt in that observation, even in jest, but there is also a nucleus of accuracy. The low pay and small size of many current congregations, coupled in some cases with geographic isolation or distance from major cities, means that fewer and fewer pastors are willing to serve—or can afford to make the sacrifices necessary to serve. All things being equal, most aspiring ministers tend to gravitate in the direction of higher pay, better benefits, a more desirable location, and the apparent prospects—at least on some level—of future growth and progress in the church.

When growth and progress aren't happening for a season, pastors may blame a variety of factors and variables. Yet if the season stretches out for a few years or longer, or if the pastor moves through several church assignments with similar outcomes, self-doubt comes creeping into the minister's mind-set.

"I'm not sure I've got what it takes to do this," Calvin tells us in the interview that opened this chapter. "I thought I did, but I'm not so sure anymore."

Charisma and Kerygma

Whether or not it's an explicitly held belief, those who serve in pastoral ministry appear to place a high degree of faith in the act of preaching or in the power of their own personal presence. They tend to believe, though perhaps in unexamined ways, that effective preaching leads to success in a church context, and/or that a charming personality (i.e., personal charisma) is the key that unlocks church growth.

This belief can become a double-edged sword. If one's personal charm (charisma) or preaching ability (doing kerygma) is what propels a church toward growth, what can be concluded when the church isn't growing? Pastors begin to doubt the person in the mirror—with varying outcomes.

When the church isn't growing, even the most accomplished speakers may doubt their effectiveness in presenting the gospel. Their previous assumptions about their gifts and graces may now be called into question. Even those with significant experience and a history of positive feedback may now wonder if they've "lost it" or "don't have it anymore" when it comes to preaching effectively. If left unchecked, this uncertainty can lead to less confidence in the pulpit, so that the performance anxiety becomes a self-fulfilling prophecy.

"I thought I could preach," David tells us as we staff the exhibit booth of a Christian publisher. "I've always had nice comments about my sermons, and my professors in seminary gave me good marks for preaching. I try really hard not to be boring, not to go long, and not to get too technical or scholarly in my preaching."

David waits until a nearby couple is out of earshot before he continues.

"My preaching ability is the one thing I've never doubted," he tells us. "When I would make a list of my gifts or my strengths, I would put preaching or teaching right near the top. Yet here I am, preaching week after week, and the people are not responding. The church is not growing. In fact, although you can't really tell it much by the numbers, we are actually losing a few people here and there.

"What am I supposed to make of that, if I'm such an effective preacher?" David asks us without waiting for our reaction. "How else should I read that kind of evidence? I mean, if I'm really preaching effectively—and I hope I am—shouldn't there be some positive feedback from the people or some positive signs in altar response, things like that? Shouldn't the church be growing, at least a little bit?"

David shrugs his shoulders.

"For the past few months, for the first time in my life, I am starting to doubt my preaching abilities." Now he lowers his volume to almost a whisper. "I haven't said that out loud to anyone, not even my wife," David says quietly. "But I lay in my bed at night, and I can't fall asleep, and I am laying there worrying about whether I've lost my gift for preaching. Or worse—maybe I never really had it."

David speaks for himself, but without knowing it, he describes the anxiety and worry of many pastors whose local churches are not in growth mode. One way or another, a decline in membership or giving or other statistics tends to fuel the flames of introspection and self-doubt. Although any number of external factors may be in play, even a highly confident pastor begins to worry about performance issues.

In Calvin's case, which opened this chapter, a local congregation had been declining for more than a decade before his arrival. Yet after three years of struggling in that same context, Calvin was wondering about himself—not the setting. He was doubting his own abilities despite accurately telling us about a church board that didn't want to contemporize their worship service and wouldn't consider relocating to attract new attenders. For a less-experienced pastor, or a more confident one, these markers in the context would indicate that the problem is not the pastor but is instead in "the people" or "the board." Yet somehow, as issues persist and numbers stay static or decline, even capable pastors begin to identify "the pastor" as the problem behind the trends.

Mark is serious as he tells us about his own experiences in this category.

"My great-aunt died in Boston," Mark recounts. "The family asked me to do her funeral, so I flew out there and preached a funeral to maybe one hundred people, all of whom appeared to be on Social

Security. It was probably the oldest crowd I have ever preached to in my life.

"What surprised me," Mark continues, "is that almost without exception, everyone attending that funeral came up to thank me for my message and tell me how much they enjoyed hearing me speak.

"I know that pastors tend to exaggerate," Mark adds, "so it's important for you to understand that I'm serious here. I don't mean that a few people or several people or even a dozen old-timers came up to thank me. I literally mean that almost everyone in that room [a chapel on-site at a funeral home] came up and personally thanked me for the message. Almost every person who attended the funeral gave me some kind of specific, kind, positive feedback about my preaching."

Mark pauses.

"Until that moment, I didn't realize how long it had been since I got a lot of positive feedback after preaching!" he exclaims. By then I'd been at my church for maybe eighteen months or so, and nothing was happening in terms of growth or outreach or success. I was still trying different things and still adjusting to a very different church culture than I was used to.

"But until that funeral," Mark relates, "I hadn't realized that the absence of positive feedback was a huge factor for me in the church I was serving. I was up there in the upper Midwest of the United States—up where people are reserved and quiet and don't express their feelings—but I hadn't really noticed their complete lack of positive response to my messages.

"Then I flew to Boston, preached a fairly routine funeral message at the service for my great-aunt, and everyone treated me like a rock star!"

Mark smiles at the memory.

"Maybe God knew that is exactly what I needed," he says. "But it also helped me identify what was missing in the church I was serving. Either my preaching was somehow subpar at the time, or my people were just unusually reserved in their way of relating to preachers. Speaking out in Boston helped me understand that I do have some gifts for preaching, and 'normal people' respond normally to my gifts."

Mark smiles again.

"So after that, I realized the problem: my church wasn't normal." He laughs. "And it may sound silly to you, but that idea really helped me. For one thing, it helped me know that I didn't want to spend my entire ministry life being a preacher in the upper Midwest, where you don't get much positive feedback. I decided that I wanted to move South or West or some other direction—anywhere where people are more expressive and responsive."

Mark sighs broadly.

"Let's face it," he says. "Preaching is a lot of work. I spend a lot more time in prayer and preparation than anyone knows or sees. So if I'm going to work that hard and put all those hours in, and I'm going to pour my heart and soul into a sermon every Sunday—I'd rather preach in front of people who are expressive of their emotions and who give positive feedback when they're happy about things.

"Preaching to a group of senior citizens in Boston was an 'aha!' moment for me and for my ministry. I came home and talked to my wife about all of this, and she told me she had been praying that I would get more positive feedback. I never knew she was doing that!

"She got really blessed when I told her how all the old people had responded to my sermon. And she was in full agreement about moving our ministry to a place where people communicate their thoughts and feelings more openly—and more often. Both of us wanted God's will—not our own—but after that funeral both of us began asking God if we could serve in a place where people smiled or laughed out loud or gave compliments from time to time—even to pastors."

Mark's processing of his own pastoral experience had not yet moved into the sphere of self-doubt or performance anxiety. And in no small measure because of the prayers of his godly wife, Mark was spared the kind of brooding introspection that leads some ministers into depression and anxiety. Instead, Mark was gifted with the chance to preach "out of context" in another location—and to discover that his gift for preaching was genuine, functional, and intact.

Not all ministers receive this same blessing. Sunday after Sunday they climb onto the platform doing their best to look confident and relaxed. Meanwhile, they are dealing with a lump in their throats, or perhaps an irregular heartbeat. As they prepare to deliver a sermon that they have carefully crafted and thoughtfully edited, they are besieged by doubts and anxieties about their own gifts. Some of this is the enemy's work, and some of it is the fruit of laboring in a type of ministry—preaching—that exposes your inner life and deepest realities.

There is something not only highly visible and but also highly vulnerable about the act of preparing and then presenting a sermon. It is a matter of baring one's soul, revealing one's identity, and exposing one's weaknesses. There is a price to pay for being in such a public ministry, regardless of the size of the church or the setting of the ministry. Preaching is more than teaching and more than explaining and more than communicating facts and ideas. It is personal, revealing, difficult, and intense. It is a struggle at all times—a gigantic struggle at some times. When self-doubt or performance anxiety begin to assault the thinking and emotions of a minister, stress levels may rise to meteoric levels.

Ask any minister how he feels after delivering a sermon, or how she feels after she has preached on Sunday morning. Ask how she feels emotionally, or how he feels physically. Have a working pastor tell you what it feels like to preach.

You may be surprised at what you hear.

5

SIGNIFICANT STRESSOR: BIVOCATIONAL COMPLEXITY

Gerald is looking forward to his new role as a DS.

"I love mentoring and training younger leaders," Gerald tells us as we lift and carry boxes from the garage to the rented moving truck. Gerald's youngest son is helping too; we've set aside a Saturday morning to help pack the truck as Gerald and his wife move across the country to begin a completely new role.

Gerald is not only excited but also realistic as he contemplates the changes that are immediately ahead. Having served for nearly two decades as pastor of several congregations, he is well acquainted with the challenges and also the privileges of pastoral ministry. For the past four years, he has been an executive in his denomination, serving and helping in a different way. His denominational service has involved nearly constant travel, most of it to meet with pastors on location.

"I've always wondered whether or not I would enjoy the superintendency," Gerald relates as we maneuver a spinet piano carefully up the ramp and onto the truck. "I guess now I'll have the chance to find out. Terry and I prayed about this, and both of us are certain that this is God's direction for the next season of our ministry. . . ."

Gerald is sanguine about the challenges—financial and otherwise—that will engage his attention in the new assignment. "More than half of the guys who serve on my district are bivocational," he tells us. "And of the remaining group, about half of those are being paid too little to survive. So in their cases their wives have fairly good jobs or good benefits or both.

"In a district of about forty churches, right now there are about half a dozen places that pay their pastor enough to live on. So maybe six churches out of forty. Do you understand the kind of pressure that puts on those other thirty-four pastors, who are serving God with gladness but can't raise their families on what the church provides by way of a salary package?"

We nod our heads knowingly. As we travel across North America and beyond, we meet with bivocational pastors on a regular basis. The bivocational pastor is increasingly normative for many districts and in many settings. As megachurches grow larger, expanding their reach and influence, midsize congregations find it more difficult to compete with the programming, the quality, and the ministry scope that these larger settings offer. Midsize churches struggle to retain their people and to maintain their identity, losing families and thus income to the larger church down the street or across town. Meanwhile smaller churches, often with paid-for buildings and a dedicated core of regular attenders, keep hanging on but can't afford to hire and pay a full-time minister. Of the jobs that become available to younger pastors, many will offer a salary that necessitates looking for a second job.

For Gerald, this is a mentoring challenge—an intriguing twist on his role as a teacher and trainer of church leaders. "I have to understand that I'll only be able to get half of the attention of these guys," Gerald tells us. "Getting together for times like ministerial training or Ministers and Mates Retreats will be a huge challenge."

Gerald is a strong advocate for women in pastoral ministry, but the district he will soon lead does not have any women serving as senior pastors. So when Gerald tells us about "the guys," he is describing his reality, not prescribing his ideals.

"If I plan something for a Saturday," Gerald continues, "maybe the guys don't have their secular jobs on that day. But understand—they haven't had the usual amount of sermon prep time during the week. If they're not working their other job on Saturday, they'll be wanting to brush up the sermon, plan the service, and do a thousand other little things to prepare for Sunday's services.

"So although Saturday may be about the only time we can offer a seminar or a workshop for these guys, I'm very aware that their time is limited—and they may not be willing to give up a Saturday when they have so little time anyway. Plus, if I grab them on Saturday for a workshop, that cuts into their time with their families. So for me, I've got to figure out some innovative ways to do teaching and training when the people I'm leading don't have any free time to give me. I may also need to rethink the idea of a Ministers and Mates Retreat—which I personally love—to accommodate the fact that these couples just can't get the time off from their mix of employers—both his and hers."

Gerald tells us these things in an excited way. He is not lamenting the changes and challenges ahead; he is looking forward to serving and helping in creative and innovative ways. "Maybe we'll use Skype for some of our workshops," he proposes. "Maybe we'll have a one-day Christmas gathering for pastors and their families—probably in November—instead of having a two- or three-day retreat in the fall, like they're used to."

As we lift and carry, perspire and converse, Gerald treats us to an impromptu discussion of the stress factors that are inherent in bivocational service. As always, we enjoy learning from him and we appreciate his wisdom.

Jesus: No One Can Serve Two Masters

Christ is teaching about money in this famous passage, yet the principle here may well be transferable across other areas and issues. It is difficult—perhaps impossible—to faithfully serve two different employers, giving allegiance to each. Life is simpler when there is only one employer and thus only one "master" to which your loyalty and faithfulness is dutifully owed.

Ask a bivocational pastor about this, and he or she is likely to laugh out loud. From the perspective of a busy, multitasking minister, there is no question about where one's primary loyalty is due.

"Hey, the church comes first," says one younger pastor at a large popular conference focused on evangelism and outreach. "My work for the school district does matter to me, and I give it my very best. But in terms of priorities or loyalties, there is absolutely no question or issue about that.

"My church is my calling. Our school district is kind enough to employ me, which helps me carry out my calling right now. I am grateful to have that option, and I hope the district feels grateful for my service to them.

"But one day, hopefully in the next two or three years, I plan to be able to de-emphasize my work for the schools and dedicate my life entirely to the church. Until then, I'm just grateful for the income that this extra job provides. Frankly, we wouldn't be making it without that additional income—my wife works, but only part-time."

Luke, who is telling us about this, serves as an on-call substitute teacher for a district with three high schools. He teaches history and social studies, and there are sometimes as many as two or three days a week when his services are needed.

"They try to let me know in advance, but a lot of times my phone rings at 5:30 or 6:00 A.M.," Luke tells us. "My wife knows if the phone rings at that time, it's for me. The central office of the district will call and ask if I can go to North High today, and if I can teach history. I keep my calendar on the nightstand because when they call, I'm usually not even awake. Before I give them a yes or a no, I check my calendar.

"The nice thing about this," Luke continues, "is that I really can say no. They don't cross me off their list or anything. I suppose if I said no a lot, maybe they would reconsider using me. But I usually say yes—I would guess that I work maybe ten days a month teaching.

"I get paid per day," he adds. "And ten days of teaching adds up to almost exactly what the church pays me for the whole month. If I could teach fifteen or twenty days a month, we could get a new car. But if I did that, I'm not sure when I'd find the time to write sermons or visit with people in the church."

We ask Luke a question about life/work balance.

He laughs easily and naturally.

"You mean work/work balance," he says gently. "I don't have a life. Right now this juggling act is succeeding for us because Julie and I haven't started our family yet. She works part-time and I work two jobs that are both kind of part-time-plus. And we can do this because neither one of us has to stay home with a baby or be home with toddlers running around all day.

"We've talked about starting a family, but both of us want to wait until the church can afford to pay me a full-time salary. We really believe that's maybe two or three years down the road—if everything goes well. When that day comes, I will quit teaching and Julie will give up her part-time job and we will start our family."

Luke is pensive for a moment.

"We'll be making less income once Julie isn't working," he says thoughtfully. "But, frankly, we're not about making a ton of money anyway. Does anybody get into pastoral ministry because they're trying to make a fortune or get rich quick? I don't think so. . . ."

We come back to our question about life/work balance.

"Julie is very understanding," Luke admits. "She can see that I'm juggling two different jobs, and she can see that we need me to do it. So when we don't have a date night, or we don't get away somewhere for a nice vacation, she knows why. She sees how hard I work putting a sermon together, and she sees me get out of bed at 6 A.M. and answer the call to go teach.

"Some wives wouldn't be so thrilled about that, but Julie is amazing," he continues. "Both of us are hoping that we can start our family in a few years and that we can enjoy more time together as a couple and also as a family. If we can really narrow our lives down from three jobs (two his, one hers) to just one job (the pastorate), we think we will have it made, in terms of family time!"

Two Jobs, One Husband and Father

Stress on the marriage is one of the first things that bivocational pastors mention when discussing the obstacles they face in ministry. Before they talk about divided loyalties and lack of rest, they tend to tell us about the difficulties at home, in the core relationship of the couple in ministry.

"I'm working two jobs, and I work very hard at both of them," one busy pastor says during our interview. "Where am I supposed to find the emotional energy—let alone the physical energy—to come home and be all romantic with my wife at the end of such a long day? I really do love her, and I think she knows that in her heart, but our life right now is not exactly chocolate and perfume."

To date, there are few, if any, reliable studies of the impact of bivocational service on perceived marital difficulties or on actual marital outcomes, such as separation or divorce. Anecdotally, although these stress factors may loom large in such cases, there is no clear indicator of a higher incidence of divorce among bivocational pastoral couples than among single-income ministers. More study is needed, but the early reports indicate similar patterns in both cohorts.

One young minister sees a parallel between his current bivocational experience and another common experience shared by couples who are starting their life together. He makes a comparison that we haven't heard elsewhere.

"It's like I'm going through med school or something," one pastor explains. "You see those couples go through med school together, where the husband or wife is studying to be a doctor and the other one works to put the spouse through school. Both members of the team—the husband and the wife—make a lot of sacrifices and put up with a lack of quality time because they are working toward a common goal. The long-term goal is bigger than their short-term marital satisfaction."

We're intrigued and explain that we haven't heard this analogy previously, although at first blush it fits well in this context.

"This is very similar," the pastor insists. "Between my two jobs, I'm probably away from the house as much as a med student would be. And when I am at home I am always studying: sermons don't prepare themselves!

"So as I see it," he continues, "it's like my wife is married to a med student right now or a graduate student working on a PhD at some Ivy League university. Our quality time is about as imaginary and scarce as their quality time would be.

"Our relationship is still solid, and it isn't going to fall apart, but both of us realize we aren't going to have our needs met right now. We aren't going to be getting much time together for romance or relaxation or intimacy. We value those things, but right now we don't have any way to achieve all that. It just can't be done.

"This is tough work," our new source explains. "Anybody who tells you differently is way out of the norms. It is very tough work to juggle two jobs, one of which involves writing sermons and preaching, and then somehow come home from one or both of those jobs and try to spend quality time with your [family]."

The busy pastor frowns for a moment.

"I'm not sure how this sounds to you," he says, checking for our reactions. "I'm not trying to depress you here, and I'm not trying to depress the people who read your book. What I'm trying to do—as best I can—is paint a realistic picture of how it goes when you are working two jobs, and one of those jobs is ministry."

Several other pastors we interview make the same connection—that a sense of shared sacrifice is essential. One adds that it's not just shared sacrifice, but it is the idea of shared sacrifice *for a limited time* that is a crucial element here.

"It's like you have unwanted guests in your house," this pastor observes. "You have company staying with you, and they've worn out their welcome, and you are just hoping and praying that they'll leave, and you can have your life back.

"You can put up with anything for a while, especially if your guests are friends or family. But what really helps is when you find out their schedule for leaving. Once you know when they're leaving, you sort of relax inside, and you start counting the days until the trouble will be over."

He stops to glance at us, making sure we are paying attention.

"So it's not just that a husband and wife are making a shared sacrifice, and they are both giving up a lot in terms of their relationship—the key is that both of them know that this is for a limited time. It matters a lot. Both of them need to have this timetable in their heads, this goal line of how long the bivocational period will continue, and how they will know when it's over.

"The idea of being a bivocational pastor for ten or twenty years—I just think that would be highly exceptional," this pastor explains. "I don't see how you could possibly have a quality marriage or a healthy family if you gave away a decade or more of your life to two employers, not one. That would be a rare case, and maybe a place where the church didn't demand much from you, or where the other job was something very mellow and noninvasive."

He sighs.

"I think a good relationship can withstand maybe a few tough years of bivocational service," he says, "but not much longer than that. I'm not trying to be unspiritual here—I hope you understand that. I'm just making some observations about human relationships. I think a good relationship can survive for a few years of sacrifice and difficulty and reduced intimacy. But sooner or later, the basic ways that a relationship grows and gets deeper are going to be the same. So if you don't start investing quality time in your marriage, you'll end up suffering for it. Your marriage won't get to the depth and the intimacy and the closeness that you want."

Since he is speaking with the voice of experience, we listen carefully.

Pulpit Envy

"I'll tell you who I have trouble with," another young pastor tells us about halfway through our short interview with him. We're sitting in an alcove just off a busy passageway at a large pastor-oriented conference. In the gaps between the afternoon workshops we are trying to schedule brief interviews with bivocational pastors. To our surprise, the number of bivocational ministers is large, even at this event. We had suspected that perhaps the bivocational servants would be unable to get away for a conference such as this one.

"Here's exactly where I struggle," the pastor continues. "As often as possible, I come to big conferences like these, and the workshop presenters are pastors of very large churches. I totally understand that reality; in fact, someday I hope to be the pastor of a very large church. To be honest with you, I'd love to be a presenter here someday too.

"But I get here, and then I start listening to these guys in some of their workshops, and I'm thinking to myself that these guys all have a secretary and they have a staff and they have people who run the volunteers who run the ministries. So these guys are at the top of the food chain, making decisions and giving orders. Meanwhile, some other people are the ones actually doing all the ministries.

"The longer I sit there, the more I struggle. I have to work two jobs or else my family can't pay our bills. I give the best I've got to my pastoral ministry, but then I have to give a lot of energy and attention to my other job! Do you think these megachurch ministers have even one iota of understanding about that? They are wise people and gifted speakers and their ideas are great—I'm always stealing good ideas from them—but do they even know what it's like to be a real-life pastor in the twenty-first century?

"These guys are a lot more like CEOs than they are like pastors," our interviewee continues. "I am so tired and so worn out at the end of my day. My wife deserves so much more time and attention than I can ever give to her. My kids need so much more face time with me than they're getting right now. And no matter which direction I look, I don't see any relief coming over the horizon. Not anywhere!"

The discussion turns personal and we do about twenty minutes of intense counseling, surrounded by other pastors hurrying to their assigned rooms. As we have noticed in other settings and situations, it is sometimes possible to achieve remarkable intimacy and privacy in the midst of large crowds. It is exactly so today.

After working through an unrelated issue and praying with this young minister for several minutes, we pause as he returns to his original topic.

"I struggle with these guys," he says in regard to larger-church pastors. "Whether it's envy or jealousy or resentment on my part, I don't know. But I sit there and wish I was one of them—and at the same time I wonder if they have any idea what it feels like to be me. Have they ever tried to change churches during a difficult season and then discovered that no other doors would open for them?

"Have they ever been paid so little salary that they couldn't feed their family? Have they ever had to go out, knock on doors, pass out résumés, and apply for any kind of work they could get? I get the feeling that these guys graduated from school, then landed somewhere right away, and over time they have stayed there and things have gone well. That is great—it's ideal, actually—but it means they've never had any 'real world' experience."

The pastor frowns.

"I guess that sounds like I believe the real world is mostly negative," he says quizzically. "That's not what I'm trying to say. I'm just saying that I'm not sure these megachurch leaders with all their books and all their Twitter followers have any idea what it feels like to be a struggling bivocational pastor who is barely getting by.

"And maybe that's where my problem is. I'm doing my best to work two jobs, and I'm not succeeding at them. I don't feel like I'm making any progress financially—I'm just treading water. I don't feel like I'm making progress with the church—we're not growing very much. I'm working as hard as I can in both settings.

"And the bottom line is this: I don't feel successful. There are no more slices of me to go around. I am already doing everything I know how to do. I am already trying everything I can possibly try. I am performing at the highest level I'm capable of, and it's not enough to make it work.

"No matter what I try, I feel like I'm not succeeding—so I'm doing my best to avoid failure."

Ministry and the "F" Word

One way or another, we hear this sentiment voiced by more than ten separate bivocational pastors at this specific conference. For these busy and tired professionals, the stress factor is not so much the existence of more than one employer. Rather, the stress is often rooted in the sense that doing one's best for two employers is not translating into noticeable "success" in either venue.

"I feel like I'm failing," one pastor sighs over a fast-food meal at our favorite SoCal burger venue. "I feel like I'm failing as a husband, failing as a father, and failing at both of my jobs. So here I am pastoring a church, working at another job because I need the money, and never home long enough to meaningfully invest in my kids or romantically invest in my wife.

"Maybe somebody else could make that work, but I can't," he concludes. "There isn't any area of my life—not any—where I feel like I'm thriving and moving forward and succeeding. I've never been this busy, and I've never tried so hard to succeed—while at the same time, I've never felt like such a failure."

We hear the "F" word from three or four of the bivocational pastors we interview here. As carefully and casually as we can, we unpack the meanings of the word by looking for metrics or markers that would validate the feelings. Instead of valid metrics, we end up with indicators that are primarily rooted in emotions.

Physically exhausted, financially challenged (more on that in the following chapter), and stretched in several directions at once, these pastors experience negative emotional baggage. They have trouble sleeping at night, tend to get sick more often, and may experience depressive thoughts across a wide range of personality and temperament varieties.

While it's true that happiness is a choice, it may also be true that failure is a feeling. Regardless of statistics or verbal input, irrespective of comments from family or parishioners, a pastor's own sense of reality may be dented or damaged by intermittent or frequent feelings of failure. When a pastor is bivocational, the additional stress factors seem to make feelings of failure more common.

Sometimes there may be symptoms in the external world that tend to validate these feelings. The church may decline in numbers or giving, or the secular job environment may provide ambiguous or negative feedback.

"I've been passed over for two promotions at work," one pastor tells us, referring to his secular career. "And they don't say it to me out loud, but I know it's because they think I have this other job to fall back on. They think I don't need the raise, or maybe they think I'm giving my first loyalty to the church. So they pass out the promotions and the raises and everybody else gets one—but not me.

"I know I'm doing a good job here, and I get good verbal feedback from my main supervisor. I've had three performance reviews since I started, and they were all mostly positive about the job I'm doing. So when I missed out on the first chance to be promoted, I didn't think much about it. But when it happened again, I started wondering if this was a pattern.

"If I wasn't doing this job while also pastoring a church, I think I would have moved up the ladder here, financially and also in additional responsibilities. But as it is, I've had to watch younger, less qualified people be promoted while I stay in the same pay grade and keep doing the same old tasks.

"I tell myself that life is unfair, and that helps a little," he adds. "But then those thoughts creep back in, and I find myself thinking that the only reason I'm not getting more money or more responsibility is that I'm dividing my time and attention between two jobs. Then I get really tempted to just walk away from the ministry, which is the lower-paying job anyway, and give my whole self to my secular employer. How much money could I be making right now if I did that?"

Meanwhile, a pastor nearing retirement age pours out his heart to us as we sip coffee with both he and his wife. The two of them are each bivocational; they work four jobs between them. As we interview them, we see signs of stress on their faces; we hear symptoms of emotional distress in their comments.

"This is my last stand," the pastor is telling us. "I've already decided that I'm too old to start all over again somewhere else. So this church is it. Either I take this church and make it self-supporting and start drawing a reasonable salary from it, or else I get out of the ministry for good. I have a part-time job with the city, and it has some benefits even though it's part-time.

"If I give up the ministry job, I can go full-time with the city. They've already told me they'll make a place for me. So in the back of my mind there is always this tantalizing possibility of quitting the ministry and going full-time in the other job.

"I want to tell you exactly how it is," he says with emphasis, as his wife reaches over to take his hand. "I would rather succeed in ministry than in any other area. I have tried to pastor faithfully and well, and this is my sixth church in about thirty years of pastoral service. I've done my best at five churches and none of them ever grew rapidly or made a lot of progress or succeeded by any other form of measurement. I can't point to any of them and show you something shiny or perfect or good, something I 'accomplished' while I was there.

"This is my sixth church to serve, and it's my last one. If something doesn't start happening around here soon, I will just hang it up and go fishing. I'll work full-time for the city and I'll have enough free time to fish all I want to. I'll be making enough money to buy myself a new bass boat. . . ."

His voice drifts off for a moment.

"I try not to think about it, but this is what haunts me all the time. I think about the money I could make and the free time I could enjoy, if I just quit pastoring and gave my full attention to the other job. I could work one job, not both."

He looks right at us, eyes moist. In the moment he seems both tired and also old beyond his years. The ministry has aged him; you can hear it in his voice.

"I would trade all of that for a chance to feel successful in ministry," he says softly and slowly. "I don't need to make money, and I don't need to go fishing. I don't need to build up a cushy retirement fund, and I don't need to buy a new boat. What I really need is to feel like my life matters and my ministry is making a difference. . . ."

He is absolutely quiet, and we do not invade his privacy. His wife, however, steps right in without waiting.

"Honey," she says with evident sincerity, "you have made a forever difference in all of the churches you've served, and you're doing it again in this one. You are being Jesus to these people and showing them how God thinks and acts and responds to human need. I see Jesus in you, and other people do too.

"You *are* making a difference," she insists in a voice that is soft yet firm. "And that is just one of the reasons I am so proud of you. I don't need money, and I don't need things. Every day of my life I am so blessed to be the wife of a godly man. You are answering God's call and you are being obedient.

"So what you are is . . . you are a success."

6
SIGNIFICANT STRESSOR: FINANCIAL SCARCITY

We arrive early for our interview, and Richard is nowhere in sight.

We park our car, stroll together into a cozy Starbucks, and quickly claim three leather armchairs set in a group near the fireplace. What are the odds that all three chairs would be empty at this moment? We sit down on two of the chairs, throwing coats and a notebook on the third chair to clearly mark it as "reserved."

Both of us are content to sit and wait here; we'll order when our guest arrives a few minutes later. Until then we are claiming the best real estate in the Starbucks—comfy chairs in front of a roaring fire. Lisa smiles at the prospect of warmth.

We are looking forward to this chance to visit with a busy pastor who is serving in pastoral ministry in the southeastern United States. We knew him a decade ago in the Pacific Northwest; since then, he and his family have completely changed not only their zip code and GPS coordinates but also their cultural context. After serving in a politically and culturally liberal portion of North America, they are now squarely in the heart of the so-called Bible Belt of the United States.

Two or three minutes before he is due, both of us notice as Richard pulls a large yellow school bus into the parking lot of the coffee-house. He maneuvers with evident skill, aligning the big bus with the far north end of the building, on an alley. His bus will not be blocking any cars; he will have an easy, drive-forward exit when he departs an hour or so later.

I compliment Richard on his driving and parking skill as he walks through the front door. His eyes adjusting to the indoor light, the bivocational minister beams brightly and has a quick answer for me.

"I'm a regular here!" he announces. "This is not the first time I've parked my bus at this Starbucks. In fact, I come here so often they almost reserve that spot for me now. I only have to move the bus if they get a delivery or something—and they try to schedule most of their regular deliveries between 10 and 11 A.M., not in the afternoon hours. Because of that, I can usually park my bus right there and leave it right there while I meet people here for coffee or counseling."

After exhausting the parking updates, we catch up on recent family news while standing in line to order our beverages. We offer Richard a muffin or biscotti; he demurs. "I'm trying to watch my weight a little bit right now," he insists. "Both of my jobs are sedentary. Either I'm sitting in my office writing my next sermon or talking on the phone, or else I'm sitting behind the wheel of a yellow school bus, driving kids to and from high school. Either way, I'm doing a lot of sitting down and not enough getting up and moving around. So until I start burning more calories, I'm trying to cut back on carbs, count calories, and maybe lose a little weight."

Richard reaches down and pats his ample stomach.

"I've lost eighteen pounds already," he says proudly. "And I'm just getting started. I really think I can lose fifty or sixty pounds by just being more careful."

While we stand together in line, Richard flips through photos of his wife and children on his iPhone, showing us a four-year-old and a two-year-old we've never met. When we knew this couple they had two daughters; they've now added yet another daughter as well as their first son, who is the youngest of their group.

"We decided to keep trying until I got my boy." Richard laughs. "I had a hard time talking Brenda into that after the third one, but she eventually changed her mind, and we kept trying."

He is grinning as he recounts their animated discussions.

"But Brenda also told me that if this fourth one wasn't a boy, I had better learn how to be satisfied with four daughters. There wasn't going to be a fifth child!" The proud father laughs again as he recalls his delight when a son was born.

"I love my girls—all three of them," the pastor insists. "But I have to tell you, it felt really special to be standing there holding my boy, a few minutes after his birth. It was different, you know? I mean, I don't love him more than I love my three girls, but there's just something about having a boy to teach and a son to raise."

Richard is obviously proud of his family and enjoys showing us the photos. He also appears to be satisfied with his prayerful choice to move away from a coastal community in Washington state, resettling his family to a small town in the rural south. What we might regard as a massive cultural shift, Richard views as an improvement in the climate—culturally as well as in terms of daily weather.

"This is such a great place to raise my kids," Richard exclaims as we listen to the sound of the froth machine, waiting for our drinks. "People here mention God all the time, and not as a swear word either. People here quote the Bible all the time. I'm in this Starbucks a lot, and I often hear other people praying with each other or talking about stuff that is happening in their church. In terms of the broader culture, this place is a much better fit with our values. We walk into a Dairy Queen here, or maybe a McDonald's, and the store is playing Christian music. We'll sit down to have some ice cream or a hamburger, and while we eat we're listening to a song by Casting Crowns. Believe me, that doesn't happen up in Washington."

Richard looks at us to be sure we understand his perspective.

"I was raised in southeast Texas," he continues, "so in a way this is like coming home for me. We're about five hundred miles from where I was born, and we're not in the state of Texas, but culturally this place feels a lot like home. I was raised in a community where most folks went to church, and even the ones who didn't go to church probably had some kind of church background in their past. There was gospel music, and there was a lot of talk about God in the regular country music too."

Richard sighs. "I was always a fish out of water up there in the Northwest," he admits freely. "I never really fit in up there. Brenda never fit either. Both of us are so much more happy down here; this place is so much more like home for both of us."

With that, our names are called: our coffees are ready. We walk over to the end of the counter and grab our drinks, and then we turn a corner and plop down into waiting chairs. The flames dance in the fireplace, the seats are prewarmed, and we're freshly equipped with steaming hot caffeine.

As good interviews go, the key ingredients appear to be in place. We're ready to interrupt the busy day of a bivocational pastor, asking him about the challenges he faces and the many ways that stress is an issue.

✳ ✳ ✳

Half an hour later, we understand where Richard's story will fit into the larger narrative of this project. Richard, despite working two jobs very steadily, is barely providing for his family's needs, by his account. He explains this to us in matter-of-fact terms, not complaining or whining.

We don't ask, but he tells us exactly what the church pays him in salary and benefits. We also don't ask, but he adds in the exact annual income he earns by driving a bus for the school district during the school year.

"I get summers off," Richard smiles. "So when the kids go home from school, I catch a break from driving the bus. I don't mind that one bit."

Adding up his two incomes Richard arrives at a number that would shock a family in a larger city—Richard and his wife appear to be living in poverty. There's no way a person could raise a family—two adults, four children—on that level of annual income. Richard admits that his income is very limited, yet he also insists that in this smaller country town, his money goes farther than it might elsewhere.

"We don't need as much here," he explains. "The cost of everything is a lot lower. Gasoline is cheaper, most groceries are cheaper, and housing is cheaper. So although I'm not making very much money, at least we're in a low-cost place to live. If we were up in Atlanta or over in Florida, we'd be completely out of luck."

Richard goes on to give us a category-by-category breakdown of where his family's income is spent each month. Again, we are not asking these things: these questions seem entirely too personal, and the topic entirely too private. We are merely hoping for a general discussion about financial stress in parsonage life. We are not trying to do an audit of a pastor's finances, now or ever.

Richard is cheerful and good-natured; he is also very transparent about money and finances. He is scribbling numbers on napkins and showing us columns for categories. A graduate of Dave Ramsey's Financial Peace University, Richard is an articulate spokesman for thrift, savings, and wise money management. Before explaining how tight things are for his family, he brings us yet another positive note about his current situation.

"When we moved here, the church kind of apologized for how little they could pay us," he remembers. "But one thing they did offer us was a one-time lump sum amount that we could use toward a down payment on a house. I had heard of churches helping pastors that way, but I was surprised when it happened to me!

"We had been living in a church-owned parsonage out in Washington, and we kind of assumed we would be doing that forever. But when we interviewed here and things were getting kind of serious, the church offered us a cash lump sum that we could use toward the down payment on our own house. The previous pastor had sold the parsonage and the church felt bad that they couldn't offer us one. So instead of helping us move into a parsonage, they offered us some help with a down payment on our own home. To us, it was a large amount of money."

The church offered the help as a loan, with a seven-year grace period before any payments would be due on interest or principal. Further, if Richard remained in the pastorate for a full seven years at that church, both the principal and interest of the loan would be entirely forgiven.

"What do they call that, a honey trap?" Richard asks us with a grin, his drawl revealing his Texas roots. "If I leave them before the seven years are up, I have to pay them back the loan; I guess probably when I sell my house. But if I stay here for seven years or more the loan just goes away. So even back then when I'm walking in the front door and saying yes to this church—what am I already thinking about? I'm thinking—hey, I better stay here for at least seven years!"

Richard smiles.

"Now that I've been here for a while, I could see myself serving out my entire ministry here," he tells us. "So you need to know that perspective before I tell you how hard it is to keep my family in groceries and to get braces and school supplies for the kids. I'm not complaining about our life here; I am trying to build something here that will be my family's foundation and home for life."

With that said, Richard is ready to talk about the financial stress he is facing.

* * *

"My wife wants to stay home with the kids until they are all in school," Richard begins. "And even if she didn't want to do that, I would want that for her. But as it is, both of us are on the same page about that idea. Both of us really value having her at home while the kids are little. Both of us really value having a parent raise our kids, instead of some day care center or baby-sitter. I know people have to make those kinds of choices all the time—they don't have any options. But if there is any possible way, we want Brenda to be home until the littlest one is in school."

So in general terms, there is only one wage earner between the two adults. This is true by common consensus and for logical (and some might say spiritual) reasons. No one is being lazy in this home. No one is a slacker here. Both adults are ready, willing, and able to work—but both value the priority of having a parent home with the younger children until they are old enough to be in school. Brenda's significant work in raising her children is acknowledged, recognized, and valued—she is employed in a high calling, working for the good of her family.

Richard's income from the church, which we will not disclose here so as to avoid causing shame or blame, is perhaps enough money for a couple to live on if they were frugal by nature and lived very simply. His church income would probably not support a couple with even one young child—let alone a family with four kids. So while Richard earns a salary for his regular job of being a pastor, he also feels the need to supplement that income by using his "free time" to earn more money.

After unsuccessfully applying for jobs at a hardware store, a department store, and a big-box retail outlet nearby, Richard was finally hired by the school district as a bus driver on the weekday high school route. He understands why the other doors didn't open, which he believes was primarily about the existence of his main role and primary employment.

"I was very open and up front with everyone as I applied," Richard tells us. "I explained to them that I couldn't ever work on a Sunday, and I explained that my pastoral work would always come first. I explained that there might be emergencies, and I might have to leave work to go take care of something. So maybe I kind of talked all those other places out of hiring me. That wasn't my goal, of course, but maybe it worked out that way overall."

By contrast, the school district job was already structured as Monday through Friday only. Occasional side trips to athletic events are optional add-ons that Richard can choose to be available for if he wishes. "Their system here is mark-on, not mark-off," Richard explains. "The drivers volunteer for those extra assignments, instead of being required to be available. So I volunteer when I can, because we definitely need the money. But also, nobody is ever expecting or requiring me to drive on a Saturday, or late on a Friday night, or whenever the games are."

When his two incomes are added together, Richard is able to make his car payment, keep his property taxes paid, and buy basic groceries for his family. The challenges are the same as those faced by many families: unexpected car repairs, routine and unexpected dental work, clothing, gasoline, heating bills, and the related expenses of family life. Not only is there no money to provide these things, but there is also a very slim margin to cover the baseline, required expenses.

"If we have one emergency every other month, we can almost handle that," Richard sighs. "But if the car breaks down one month, and then somebody chips a tooth during the next month, we're in trouble fast. The only way to solve that would be to start putting everything on credit cards.

"We refuse to do that. Once you start going down that road, there is no going back from it. We may be poor—well okay, we actually are poor—but we are not going into debt. We are not going to burden ourselves or our kids with loans to credit cards or banks or to anyone else.

"One of the best things we learned in Financial Peace University is the freedom and joy of being free of debt. It's a mantra for us now. We paid off our student loans and we paid off some other loans, and we have no revolving debt at all. We have a mortgage on our house, but equity in it. We are making a payment on our car, but we only have about a year left to pay it off. We will only borrow for a major purchase like a house or a car—no credit cards, no other kinds of loans."

Richard is resolute and almost defiant in tone. It's clear that for he and Brenda, debt is a negative idea and a "solution" that is off the table permanently. For both Richard and Brenda, debt is a problem rather than a solution.

"We won't go there," Richard insists while talking about using credit cards to pay the dentist or the auto repair shop. "Maybe in the most dire emergency you could imagine, but even then I hope not. We do have a credit card, but it's there as a safety net that we hope we never, ever use."

✳ ✳ ✳

For more than three decades, pastors making the choice to leave ministry have cited financial stress or financial scarcity as a primary or very important factor in their decision. Faced with the prospect of perpetually limited resources, pastor after pastor has eventually decided that "as for me and my house" we will go find another way to earn a living, something that pays more and has better prospects.

The logic of this thinking does not escape Richard's attention.

"I know I could make a lot more money doing other things," Richard says, then sighs. "Anybody can see that. My brother-in-law has a car dealership over in Tampa, and he always tells me I would make a great car salesman. I actually think I might enjoy doing that, and sometimes while I'm driving the bus I daydream about that.

"He tells me what his top salesmen are earning every month and I can't believe it. They make great money, and all they do is drive cars and talk to people all day," Richard exclaims. "How hard can that be? It sounds like a dream job."

One by one, Richard lists the names of four friends he attended seminary with, each of whom has left the ministry since graduation—a little more than a decade ago. Ten years after these five suited up in robes and mortar boards, only one of them is still serving in a setting of congregational ministry. Four of the five seminarians have found other work instead.

"One of them probably shouldn't have been a pastor," Richard believes as he reviews the list with us. "He just wasn't suited for the emotional pressure of this role. He was more of a teacher type. He thought he could just explain Hebrew words and teach theology, and everything in the church would work out fine."

"The other three guys are pretty much like me," Richard explains. "All of us graduated together and we all realized we wouldn't be making a fortune as pastors. I mean, who doesn't understand that, even as a seminarian? We knew what we had signed up for, and we were ready for it, even excited about it.

"But those guys got out there, and they got into churches about the size of mine, and they ended up deciding that they wouldn't ever be able to feed their family. They ended up deciding that they wouldn't ever make progress financially unless they changed careers. So out of five of us that were good friends in our school days at seminary, I'm the only one who is still on duty as a pastor.

"What does that tell you about how things are for pastors?"

Full-Time Job, Part-Time Pay

A busy and experienced DS agrees to chat with us about the financial pressures that today's pastors are facing in ministry. He ticks off the list of churches in his area of service, dividing the group between those churches that pay what he calls a "reasonable" salary—meaning enough to feed one's family—and those churches that can only offer a portion of a reasonable salary.

By his math, this sage leader explains that more than two-thirds of the congregations on his district are offering what he calls "part-time pay for a full-time job leading the church." He says this without evident sarcasm or cynicism, without any tone of bitterness or accusation. He explains these facts the way a college professor might present a lecture—fair, balanced, and unemotional.

He sees at least two aspects of the issue that are worth noting.

"For me, it's a recruiting issue—almost daily," he tells us. "I'm out there making the phone calls or visiting with students at [a Christian university] and I'm trying to get them interested in serving on my district.

"So I tell them about our leadership climate, and I describe to them the ways I try to teach and train pastors on my district. We do a lot of continuing education, and I bring in speakers and consultants any chance I get. I honestly believe that our district is a great place for a young minister to grow up, to get trained, and to become the leader that God wants him or her to be.

"But sooner or later it comes down to cases. If I'm pitching an offer to someone, it comes down to a church and where it is located. Then it comes down to whether or not the church has any housing to offer. And finally—although it's not usually the last item in terms of priority—it comes down to how much of a salary package the church can put together."

The seasoned executive leans back in his chair before continuing.

"At first I had to learn not to blush while telling people the salaries," he says with a wry expression on his face. "The financial numbers were just so low. I would sit there talking with a prospect, but the whole time I would be wondering whether I'd want my son or daughter to start somewhere at this rate of pay. And you already know the conclusion of that: of course I wouldn't want my son to work this cheap! Of course I would want my daughter to be taken care of a lot better financially if she was interviewing to accept a new church assignment.

"So at the same time—while I'm pitching a church to a prospect—I'm thinking to myself that the salaries are so low, I would never want my own son or daughter to accept such a place. Call that a double standard if you will, but what was I supposed to do? Stop pitching churches to prospects? Stop visiting the campus of [a Christian university] for recruiting purposes?

"I had five or six churches a year that would come open and need to be filled," he continues. "So I was always prospecting. I always kept a stack of files on my desk that were prospects for churches on my district. When times would slow down, I would go through the stack and order them in terms of how I saw them: from the one I would try to recruit first, down to the bottom of my pile. But I was always recruiting, always looking for prospects, almost always having to give someone the bad news about how little they would be paid, if they said yes."

He leans back again and purses his lips.

"So first of all, it's a recruiting challenge for me," he recaps. "On a regular basis I have to recruit new pastors to serve, even though the local congregations can't pay those men and women enough salary to live on. I feel the tension of that every day, not just when I'm meeting new candidates. I talk to my wife about that frequently, and both of us wonder what we would do if we were just starting our careers right now, instead of being near the finish line."

In a moment, the superintendent turns to his second point.

"The other issue, which has nothing to do with me, is how difficult it is for young pastors to graduate from school, and maybe have some loans to pay back from their college or seminary years, and they take a job that doesn't pay enough money to live on. They can't even cover the basics, let alone pay back all of those loans. At least when you graduate from medical school, you expect to get a job that will make it simple to pay back those loans.

"But with pastoring, how long will it take? I talk with men and women who are graduating from Christian colleges who have eighty or even one hundred thousand dollars in student loans that need to be paid back. And these are students who haven't even attended graduate school yet!

"How are they supposed to repay any of those loans? How are any of them supposed to move forward and plan for their financial futures, when they can't even go down to Walmart and buy the food they need to feed their children?"

He is silent for a moment, letting the question hang in space.

"So financial scarcity has at least two issues in it," he summarizes. "For me it's a recruiting challenge, almost daily. And for the men and women who serve on my district, or who consider serving on my district, it is a bleak prospect that there may not be a way to build their financial future by serving a congregation.

"Some of this may be the global economic downturn," he muses. "I suppose that might be a factor here. But I think the bigger picture, at least for churches, is that numbers are declining and giving is declining, and there just aren't resources to offer to prospective pastors.

"One thing this means, for the local church, is that they may need to get used to the idea of having a very young minister who is just starting out or else having a pastor who also works at another job. It is going to get harder and harder for many of my churches to hire a competent, experienced, professional pastor.

"I hear people complain about our denominational budgets all the time," the same leader continues. "But I'm not sure that's where the issue is. In fact, I think that the new approaches to budgeting are giving almost too much relief to the churches. Maybe they should be investing a lot more in missions than they do now.

"Meanwhile, I think in the broader picture the issue is not really budgets at all. The real issue is that we're not paying our pastors enough to live on, reasonably. We need to step back, maybe even hire a consultant or something, and do a study about how to support our pastors, train our pastors, and then give them the hope of a lifetime of serving the church.

"If we don't do that—and soon—we are going to keep on losing our best and brightest to other types of work, instead of ministry," he concludes. "And every time a bright young pastor—or maybe a more experienced one—decides to leave the ministry, I think that's a tragedy.

"For every minister who flames out by making a big mistake, there are maybe eight or ten others who check out, giving up because they can't make a living."

He fixes his gaze directly at us.

"Is that what we want for the future of our Zion?"

7
SIGNIFICANT STRESSOR: SITUATIONAL ADVERSITY

Think of it as the Hatfields versus the McCoys.

Or for those of you with a more literary bent, consider this narrative as similar to the long-standing feud between the Capulet family and their sworn enemies the Montague family. Bill Shakespeare knew what he was talking about; once people decide they don't like each other, they create a lot of momentum for that hatred. Sometimes that momentum carries forward for generation after generation.

So it was here. This was like the popular show "Family Feud" without the genial host, the points on the board, or the valuable cash and prizes. Overall it was more like "Call of Duty"—the war game.

When Martin ("Mack") arrived to serve his next assignment, he didn't know that he was stepping right into a shooting gallery. He had no idea that open warfare was going on in his new church. And although the bullets weren't directly aimed at him—at least, not as he arrived—there was a lot of collateral damage happening out there on the battlefield.

The church was at war: it was family versus family, group against group. There were two camps, two mind-sets, two sets of people hoping to either hold on to their control or else somehow gain control of the church and its future. Not only were things tense, but there was an undeclared war between the two opposing factions.

"It's the kind of thing I would have really liked to know about, before I agreed to pastor this church," Mack tells us with a weary smile. "You know, the kind of basic information that might have been included when they were telling me about it."

Mack's smile turns downward into a frown.

"I don't know if the superintendent was unaware, or maybe he knew of the drama but underestimated it," he continues. "I'm guessing the previous pastor must have mentioned something about all of this as he was leaving. I try not to just assume that, but it seems so likely that my predecessor would have said something to someone. I doubt if he just left without explaining himself.

"So if the previous pastor did say something about all of this, and if the superintendent had been meeting with this unruly assortment of people—then why didn't I get some kind of a clue while I was praying about it or while my wife and I were flying out there for a visit or before we seriously considered taking our two kids out of school and going over there to accept this new position?"

It's a mostly rhetorical question, and we leave it unanswered.

Mack sits back in his chair, composes his thoughts, and then resumes a narrative about situational adversity and its impact on pastoral stress.

In the case of Mack's new congregation, the two warring factions were split along lines that may be quite familiar to experienced ministers and congregational leaders. On one side was a key family whose various members held the positions of church treasurer, church board secretary, and chairman of the church board of trustees. So, in effect, the major power positions of the church were all being filled by members of one large extended family. Most of the rest of the church board was populated with long-term friends and allies of this family.

So far as Mack could determine by a quick review of church records, this same family had been in control, one way or another, for more than a decade. He suspected they might have been controlling the church for an even longer period of time. Their control had survived at least three pastoral changes and had endured through a variety of church mission statements, discussions about relocating to a new setting, and other issues of church life.

This powerful faction mostly wanted the church to maintain the status quo. This group was constantly concerned about painting the building, buying new carpet for the foyer, adding gutters to the educational unit, and similar issues. When this faction talked about "church needs," they were almost always dealing with the physical plant and what they saw as a need to upgrade or renew church facilities.

The other group, holding no significant church offices and having only one lone member on the church board, was comprised of what Mack terms "Celebrate Recovery" people. Mack uses the term with much affection: he is referring to people with messy lives—and sometimes also messy personal habits—who have a genuine encounter with Jesus Christ and then begin to attend a local church. Mack loves this group with all his heart, but as he'll insist later in the interview, he did not get involved in taking sides or choosing favorites. He was still fairly new to serving as a pastor, and he was brand-new to this specific congregation—but he was wise enough to know that taking sides or choosing favorites would doom his ministry.

The second faction, whom Mack secretly preferred, was focused on issues such as outreach and evangelism. This group of people had a tendency to get very frustrated when the financial resources of the church were being invested in what they saw as trivial material things, such as paint and carpet. "We ought to be reaching more people," this group would hold as a mantra. "We ought to be out there, going where the lost people are."

This informal and ad hoc faction held relatively little political power in the church, but numerically was about the same size as the group containing the controlling family and their key allies. So in terms of sheer numbers, each faction had about the same amount of adherents. But in terms of power and control, one side held virtually all of the authority and decision-making ability, while the other faction had almost no input into church decisions, especially financial choices.

Meanwhile, what began as philosophical differences and varying opinions about church priorities had somehow become all-out warfare. Both factions were firmly entrenched; both factions had decided that "the other group" was the problem and needed to be urged, eased, or booted out of the church. Things had moved beyond politely managed anger, beyond passive-aggressive tendencies. By the time Mack unpacked into the parsonage, the two opposing factions made little secret of their total disgust with each other.

"We need to throw out the whole church board," Mack remembers the second faction telling him fairly soon after he arrived. "We will never make any real progress as a church, so long as the [name of family] are in control around here. They keep all the money to themselves and they treat it like it is their own.

"All they care about is how the lawn looks, whether the carpet is new, and how much money we have available to spend on more and more remodeling," one member of this faction claimed. "All they care about is that kind of nonessential stuff—they don't care about people at all. They don't care about the lost. They don't care about the people that Jesus came to save—Jesus died to save!"

Mack, listening without comment, noticed the use of the word "they" to describe the opposing faction. It was one of his early insights into the divisive nature of the ongoing feud between the two groups.

The other group was vocal in its perspective also.

"Pastor," one member of the lead family said to Mack, "all of us are really glad that people are finding Jesus and coming to church. That's just great. But when you find Jesus and start living for him that ought to mean that you quit smoking and you quit swearing and you start cleaning up your act. You don't hang on to those old ways. You start growing up in Jesus, you know? And if you aren't growing up in Jesus and you aren't changing your old ways, doesn't that kind of call into question whether you really belong to Jesus in the first place?

"Pastor," this person continued, "what we really need is for you to preach some messages about what happens when you follow Jesus. People need to be held accountable for the habits and their behaviors and the way they talk. If not, we are just watering down the message and letting anybody come to church."

As Mack recalls it, that woman's perspective was one of the nicer and kinder ways in which the controlling family talked about those who were in the opposing faction. At other times, the outsider faction was given emotionally charged labels, such as *ungodly* or *unchristian*. And at all times the key argument of the controlling family seemed to be that "we need to stand for something around here" or "we need to uphold the standards of this church so that everyone knows what they are."

When they spoke about the standards of this church, Mack discerned that this faction was talking about rules, social customs, and personal behavioral issues. Nobody was attacking or defending Wesleyan or Arminian thought; no one was arguing on behalf of Reformed theology or a Calvinist perspective.

This was not a Wesley versus Calvin situation. This was the Hatfields on one side, shooting at the McCoys on the other.

✳ ✳ ✳

Mack believed that his wisest course of action was to not take sides. Meanwhile, he did his very best to serve as an honest broker between the two opposing camps. He was new to church conflict, and he recalls being very glad that whatever the problems were, they didn't involve him.

His optimism—or perhaps his naive perspective—was short-lived.

"In my heart I definitely sided with the second group," Mack admits. "I've never gotten very excited about all-church painting days or similar projects. While we spend all our time sprucing up our own nest, other people are going to hell—literally. So in my heart there was never any question. I love the perspective and the values of the second group—which doesn't mean that I agreed with their being at war or that I gave them a pass for having bad attitudes about church leaders."

Mack stayed studiously neutral, listening closely to each side and doing his best to help each side see the positive virtues of the other.

"I don't have a lot of training in psychology or sociology," Mack explains. "But I've always believed in trying to create a win-win situation where everybody gets something they want. So I came into this, completely unaware of the depth of the divisions and the scope of the problems, just wanting everyone to be at peace. I was hoping to create a win-win here. My goal was to satisfy everybody, but I ended up alienating both sides. I can see that now, but I didn't see it coming back then."

After realizing that he was in a very challenging situation, Mack decided to reach out to someone he believed he could trust, someone he believed would have either the positional authority or the relational wisdom to add significant help.

"I'll keep the names and personalities out of this," Mack tells us. "But I turned to the one person I thought might really be able to help me. I also thought he might know more of the background of what was going on here. I kind of regarded him as an older, wiser minister and also as a resource person who could give me some useful wisdom."

Mack smiles, looks down at his feet, then slowly continues his story.

"He listened to me very patiently for maybe a half hour," Mack remembers. "Then when it was all said and done, he told me to always pay attention to whose signature was on my paycheck."

Mack says this with emphasis, and then is silent.

"That was pretty much exactly what he said. He didn't give me any tips on conflict resolution or how to defuse tension or anything else. He listened really well, or at least I thought he did, and then all he said was to notice whose signature was on my checks. In other words—and maybe I assumed this is what he meant—I should be on the side of the people with the money.

"He was sort of implying that if I wasn't on their side, I could lose my job. At least that's what I assumed he meant by that statement. Does any other explanation make sense? I sat there kind of stunned that he would have that perspective.

"Does controlling the money in the church make someone right?

"Does controlling the money in the church make someone the person whom the pastor should automatically support or agree with?

"I had no response to him, that day," Mack continues. "Maybe I had built up too high of expectations of what I might hear or what he might tell me. Maybe I held his office in too high of esteem. All I know is, I walked away from that meeting kind of in shock, kind of not believing what I had heard.

"And as I drove home, the major feeling I had was that I was in this alone. There wasn't anybody who was going to come riding in on a white horse and either rescue me or give me good advice. I was on my own—I had to find my own way to get through this.

"Mostly, I felt abandoned and alone," Mack sighs. "And that's why I want to keep personalities and identities out of this discussion. It doesn't matter who made me feel that way. I am just trying to tell you what I felt, in the middle of one of the worst crises I had ever faced as a pastor."

Conflict and Casualties

James is a thoughtful, scholarly looking graduate student who is pursuing his doctorate at a seminary in the Southeast. Among several topics that interest him, he has chosen to do his doctoral dissertation on the ways church conflict can play into a pastor's decision to leave the ministry.

"I've been finding two different kinds of decisions that pastors are making," James tell us in the cafeteria of his graduate school. "One is a decision to leave that particular place of ministry—to flee the conflict and find a new place to serve. This seems to be a fairly common reaction to a church in conflict. A pastor will try to solve or resolve the issues, but if things don't improve, the minister will often begin to call people, go to his network, and look for a new place to serve.

"The other kind of decision, the one I am primarily studying, is a choice to leave the ministry as a vocation and to enter some other line of work. There is no clear trend among this group as to where they gravitate after being pastors," he continues. "Some are moving over into the chaplaincy, some are looking for work as denominational executives, and many are running away from the arena entirely, taking up secular work in information technology or sales or in fields that are completely different from their prior roles in pastoral settings."

James studies his notes before continuing.

"I am studying the second group, but I keep finding people in the first group that want to make comments or give input. So I listen to them and I try to be helpful, but my focus in my project is to study persons who left pastoral ministry because of conflict in the congregation. And among this group—the second group—I am hearing two or three very common themes."

As James and many others articulate these themes, they are:

1. Conflict is hurting my family

Pastors in this cohort believe that in order to protect their families, they would be wise to leave pastoral ministry and find jobs that are less damaging to family health and wellness. These pastors talk about how the struggles in the church have made negative impressions on their children or have hurt the feelings of their spouses.

"I'm not willing to put my family through this anymore," James quotes one pastor as telling him. "I need to get them out of this situation before they lose their faith or before they quit believing that church is a good idea and that Christians love each other.

"If I stay here much longer, my kids are going to think that all Christians ever do is fight and yell at each other. How can I put my kids into that model and show them that kind of Christianity? The longer they see that, the less likely they are to want to be Christians. So at least for me, the solution is to get out of pastoral ministry and look for a healthy church where we can just attend the services and my kids can be in the youth group, and hopefully they will have a more positive view of things."

James tells us that when talking about conflict in the church, the pastors he interviews will quickly discuss how the conflict is impacting their own marriages or their own families.

For this cohort, the decision to leave pastoral ministry is a self-protective mechanism aimed at improving family life and/or marital health.

2. This is not a good fit for who I am

Pastors in this group experience extended conflict within their parish or congregation, then reflect on whether or not they are suited for duties of pastoral care—in terms of their core gifts, temperaments, and personality types. These pastors may enter the ministry with an appropriately strong sense of self, yet the existence of unresolved conflict eventually weakens their personal security.

"I feel like if I'm going to succeed as a pastor, I have to be some sort of mediator or peacemaker," one pastor tells James. "And that's just not who I am. I love studying God's Word, and I love teaching God's Word. Theology is probably my favorite subject out of any. I love reading the early church fathers and trying to learn from their perspectives. I enjoy the arguments about faith versus works or salvation by grace alone or things like that.

"I entered pastoral ministry to try to help people understand who God is, how his kingdom works, how to be rightly related to God," this former pastor continues. "That's how I am wired, and that's what I enjoy doing. So I entered the ministry with a lot of hope about educating people and helping people understand God. For example, although I don't always agree with him theologically, I love the way John Piper writes such straightforward, clear expositions of biblical truth.

"About two years into trying to be a pastor," this ministry veteran explains, "I realized that being a parish minister meant holding people's hands, listening to them cry about things, and getting caught in the middle when people were fighting with each other. And at least in [name of church], people were fighting all the time.

"There I was, hoping to enlighten people and help them find the right pathways to God, and all they wanted to do was fight. And they kept wanting me to validate them and affirm them and join their side of the fight or the argument. All they cared about was whether or not I would support them against the 'evil' people on the other side of the discussion.

"I hung in there as long as I could, maybe too long. But eventually I realized that I would be better off in the classroom, teaching students at a college or seminary. That's how God put me together. I am not a hand-holder or a personal counselor or a peacemaker or a mediator. I am a student of the truth and a teacher of the truth.

"That's what I care about. That's who I am."

Within this cohort, one encounters men and women whose experience of conflict confirmed that they were not really suited for ministry settings. Tiring of constant relational dysfunction and weary of mediating the struggles among various factions, persons in this cohort began to conclude that a classroom or a hospital or some other venue of service might be a better fit. Over time, they took steps in these directions, eventually leaving behind pastoral service as a vocation.

3. I am losing my faith in ministry (or perhaps also in God)

Among persons leaving pastoral ministry, a third segment is comprised of men and women whose views of ministry as a vocation have now changed—in primarily negative ways. These former optimists have decided that pastoral service is an impossible or untenable situation or that the church (globally speaking) is not living out the faith in ways that are health-giving and wise.

"I'm ready to be part of a house church," says one person from among this cohort. "I was never entirely sure I believed in a paid minister anyway, just as a concept," he continues. "But after trying to serve that way for several years, and just constantly watching conflict and fighting and trouble and disaster breaking out—I wonder if we need to have paid referees instead of paid ministers.

"I'm ready to be in a small circle of believers, where we are all equal and we all share each other's burdens," this respondent continues. "We used to talk about this when I was in seminary, and we talked about it in kind of ideal terms. I hadn't really worked through how I felt about it by the time I said yes to my first (and only) pastoral assignment.

"But right now, that's what I need. I need a setting where I am not the leader and people don't come running to me every time their feelings get hurt or someone attacks them or they disagree with a church decision. I'd rather sit around somebody's living room and pray, sing some worship songs, and get to know each other's hearts at a deep level.

"This is what John Wesley was all about," insists this respondent, "when he invented the whole idea of people growing up spiritually by meeting together in small groups for prayer, fellowship, and accountability. I have tried to be all things to all people—and the result is that I wasn't very helpful to anyone.

"I am losing my faith in pastoral ministry as a vocation. I am not going to blame or judge other people who believe God is calling them to that. Maybe he is. But I wonder whether God is really calling us to get into small groups, tell each other the truth, confess our sins, and pray for each other. Talk and pray, read Scripture and worship, learn and grow.

"That is what calls to my heart right now. That is where God is taking me on my journey with him. I don't know where—or even if—I am going to find it, but at least I know what I'm looking for."

For others in this cohort, the loss of faith goes deeper than losing faith in a method or a process or a way of doing "church" as a group. For these, the problem is more at the core—the existence and nature of God.

"I'm not ready to say I am a nonbeliever," admits one interviewee. "But I'm ready to admit I have serious doubts about God. I haven't turned in my credentials or told my family what I think. I am keeping this to myself while I reflect on everything. I am not jumping to any conclusions here.

"But I am really tired of being around God's people. The longer I try to serve a church full of carnal, selfish, conniving, conflicted people, the more I doubt whether there really is a God. I mean, if there is a God, why doesn't he take a more active interest in cleaning house?

"I know this sounds like I'm holy and other people aren't. I am not saying that. I know I'm not holy—but maybe that's the point. I am tired of trying to pastor people who believe they are holy—when the opposite is true.

"Here is what I do mean: some of the cruelest, meanest, most petty, and vindictive people I have ever been around were not only in the church but were leaders in the church. They honestly believed they not only were God's people—but were also 'insiders' or kind of special.

"I have looked at that and looked at that and looked at that. And at the end of the day, I am wondering to myself whether there really is a God."

From raw emotions like these we can draw a better understanding of life in the pastoral arena, as men and women cope with bad behaviors, bad attitudes, and just plain bad people. Those who doubt the fallen nature of humanity have probably not tried to lead or serve a human organization.

Loyalties Gone Wild

Another source of church conflict emerges when one pastor or staff member gains a personal following at the expense of corporate or collective unity. Whatever the role or specific assignment of this individual may be, he or she gathers a cadre of disciples who are loyal to the person rather than loyal to Christ, devoted to the cause, or passionate about the greater good of the congregation.

Working pastors can supply numerous examples of this problem, from among their own experiences and also from the encounters of others in ministry.

At a large congregation in the Southwest, the primary worship leader was a charming, highly charismatic personality with many gifts. While leading worship he might stop and give his personal testimony or perhaps quit singing and tell a story from his own life. He would do this as an indication of "getting blessed," but there were those who wondered if he planned his blessed encounters in advance.

No one knew.

The person had served in this highly visible role throughout the duration of two previous lead pastors. It is not clear whether the conduct of this staff member impacted the decision of two ministers to leave this setting and serve elsewhere. What can be known is that when the third lead pastor arrived, conflict emerged almost immediately.

"When it was time for worship on Sunday morning, [name] let me know that he was in charge of the show," says the third lead pastor (now departed from the setting and serving gladly in another location). "No matter how many times I would set up an order of service or establish our direction for the Sunday morning experience, [name] would just do whatever he wanted.

"He would nod his head in meetings, and he would take the little sheet of paper I would give him with an order of service on it. But when the music began and the service started, he was in complete control. He did whatever he wanted to do, in whatever order he wanted to do it. He had the service completely in his own hands and he just ran with it. Clearly, he had been doing that for a long time.

"Often, he would cloak this in the guise of getting blessed," the former pastor explains. "He would get the people all stirred up with a great solo—and let's face it, the guy could really sing—then under the guise of getting blessed he would tell yet another story that made him look and sound like a spiritual giant, like this big hero of the faith.

"After the first two or three times he did that, the pattern was very clear. His little stories were not about God or about giving glory to God. His stories were always about how he was the hero over here or the servant over there or the stunning solution to someone's emergency in yet another place.

"Story after story, he basically told us how great he was. And although the sharper people caught on to that, most people were so busy getting 'blessed' that they didn't really stop to evaluate what was happening. They were just riding this whole emotional experience that the guy could create. He was a master at that."

The former pastor tells us a personal anecdote that will remain unshared.

"He could not have been more personally disrespectful of my leadership or my authority," he says as we return to the primary topic. "In a staff meeting he would be polite and he would nod his head, and if you didn't know better you would think everything was great. But then when the big Sunday show started, he would just throw our order of service out the window and ignore whatever we had decided in staff meeting, and he would just run the show his way, in his timing.

"He was this huge problem, and I didn't know how to solve it," says the third pastor to depart from this setting. "I couldn't say anything against him, and I didn't feel free to remove him from his role as the worship leader. If I had tried that, I think there would have been a big congregational revolt.

"Our people worshipped this guy—and that was the problem," the sage minister continues. "And although I noticed it right away and tried to work my way through it as best I could, in the end I couldn't figure out any way to solve it. So instead of finding a solution, I chose to find the exit.

"Honestly I wonder if my two predecessors did the same thing," he opines. "I've never had the courage to ask them, and I'm not sure they'd be honest with me anyway. Whenever we leave a place, we pastors always have holy-sounding reasons and plausible explanations.

"But I'm telling you the truth—I left because I couldn't figure out how to have a viable ministry in that setting. I probably should have fired the guy before I left, like those presidents who pardon people on their last day in office. Maybe I should have tried that kind of maneuver, but frankly, I was just ready to get out of there.

"I stayed for a reasonable amount of time—so I couldn't be accused of being a quitter—and then I got out of there. I don't know how things are going there now, and frankly, I don't care. In my current ministry I have a worship leader who is Spirit-filled and who listens not only to the Holy Spirit but also to the lead pastor. Wow, I can't tell you how great that feels, after doing three years of highly conflicted ministry."

The staff member in this situation was not directly leading a revolt *against* the senior pastor; instead he was leading a cult of personality aimed at centralizing his own power and influence among the congregation, at the expense of the man the congregation had called and installed in senior leadership. Open rebellion was unnecessary so long as this worship leader held the upper hand during public celebrations of worship and praise.

In other settings and situations, the cult of personality erupts into open warfare against the senior pastor, with casualties on many fronts. Many a lead pastor has lost his standing in the congregation as a result of concerted efforts to undermine or question his character, gifts, or fitness for the role. The cult of personality is a particularly vexing type of organizational cancer, which if left unchecked can quickly contaminate the entire body.

"I had a youth pastor who was openly contemptuous of my ministry, and I didn't know it for a long time," one minister tells us. "He was very polite and nice to my face, and in meetings he would often compliment what I said or affirm my point of view in a discussion. In retrospect—and I admit I didn't see it at the time—he was behaving like the character Eddie Haskell in that old show *Leave It to Beaver.*

"He was very nice to me, very affirming in meetings, and I trusted that," the pastor continues. "Until the Friday night that I slipped in the back for a youth event, standing along a back wall in a nearly dark gym. It was not my pattern to attend these events, and no one expected me to be there.

"I showed up, and I listened, and he was basically mocking the sermon I had preached the Sunday before," the pastor continues. "He didn't put it like that. He said 'some people would say that . . .' and then he quoted from my message. And after quoting me directly he would point out how foolish the reasoning was or how simplistic the argument was or how true faith was not that way at all.

"I just stood there in the background, hidden in the darkness, and I could not believe what I was hearing! The same guy who had been so nice to me in our staff meeting on Wednesday was completely cutting up my sermon on Friday night, telling the teens not to believe what I said, not to trust what I told them.

"Again, he didn't say that explicitly—he just directly quoted the sermon we all heard the previous Sunday—my sermon—and then shot holes in it. He kept shooting and shooting until everything I said in my sermon was fully shot down."

The pastor pauses, the pain of the experience still fresh in his memories.

"I had to decide whether or not to fire him," he continues. "And the more I thought about it, I didn't see any good public reason I could give for firing him. So I simply quit trusting him and started looking for ways to get him out of our church. About six months later I had someone call me and ask about him, and without directly lying, I gave him a glowing review, focused on strengths he did have.

"Sure enough, he got a job offer from a larger church, and he was gone," the pastor said, then sighed. "So my problem was solved. And I'm not proud of my weakness or my lack of courage, but I couldn't figure out any gracious way to fire him without the teens or their parents all coming after me.

"So I recommended him right out of our church, and into a bigger one. Will God forgive me? Will his current lead pastor forgive me? I guess I can't actually be sure he is the same way up there that he was with me.

"But after he was gone, I had about a half-dozen people, some of them members of our staff, who came and told me that this guy had gossiped about me and slandered me behind my back, almost constantly. He had a cynical and sarcastic sense of humor, and I knew that. But not until he was gone did I discover that behind my back, I was often a target of that sarcasm."

The pastor finishes his narrative with a question.

"If he hadn't taken another job, what would I do?" he wonders. "Does our church manual have 'insubordination' or 'disrespect' as a category for dismissing a staff member? Wow, I hope I never have to find out. Meanwhile our new youth guy only has one face, so to speak. He is just as nice to me behind my back as he is polite and respectful to me in person. . . ."

The Exodus

In one of the better surveys of church stress and its impact on pastors, Fuller Seminary asked pastors how many had considered leaving the ministry as a vocation within the past three months. Fifty percent of respondents—half of those surveyed—had done so. And seventy percent of those responding reported having a lower self-image than they had when they began their pastoral service.

Meanwhile many pastors leave their current assignments and go elsewhere, while many others leave ministry entirely and choose to engage in other types of vocations and careers. At the time of this writing, a new study reveals that some 1,700 persons depart from pastoral ministry each month. For many of these, the existence of situational adversity—usually some type of conflict in the church—is a key factor in their decisions.

SECTION THREE
STRATEGIES THAT CAN REDUCE MINISTERIAL STRESS

INTRODUCTION

In this section, we will try to accomplish two primary objectives. Within the first chapter of this section, we will address the concepts and ideas that drive today's stress-resistant pastors. As it turns out, these busy men and women share some core ideas, beliefs, and practices that are interesting and relevant to our discussion.

We'll review five of these core ideas and values, with an explanation about the "how" and the "why" for each one. You'll discover that stress-resistant pastors tend to be highly focused on the big picture, regarding the overall objective as the main thing, and other issues as tangential, peripheral, or even trivial. You may learn that you share some of these core values—if so, you are already on your way to increasing your stress resistance and surviving the traumas of pastoral ministry.

In the second chapter of this section, we will get extremely practical, with a review of four habits that other pastors and spouses have used in order to de-stress their lives, unwind a bit, and begin to enjoy life more. Although we received more than a dozen basic categories of suggestions, these four were "drivers" that were mentioned frequently—and some of them derive also from our own experience as counselors to pastors, missionaries, and those who serve in ministry.

For this second chapter, there was a secondary mission to focus on ideas that are essentially free or cheap. If a stress-reducing strategy is expensive or otherwise unobtainable, it hardly matters how effective it might be. Our focus is on identifying and clearly explaining some key habits that you could use in your everyday life—at a cost that any ministry couple could afford.

So, driven by core values, practical concerns, and an underlying desire to find and deploy "cheap" ideas, we present the next two chapters, in which we focus on why and how to reduce your stress while serving in pastoral settings.

Happy reading—and may you find God's grace near you and with you.

8
FIVE SECRETS OF
STRESS-RESISTANT PASTORS

Given the highly stressful nature of some types of employment—emergency room nurse, police officer, pastor—why do some
persons apparently thrive and succeed in these intensely stressful
environments and situations, while others tend to flame out or fade
out? Since anyone serving in these roles faces negative stress and its
dangerous consequences, why are some able to avoid becoming the
victims of stress? How do some manage to emerge victorious despite
the never-ending onslaught of difficult circumstances and significant challenges?

Since this book is addressed to clergy, let's localize the question.

Why do some pastors burn out and leave parish ministry, while
others—who may experience similar or even higher levels of stress
and adversity in their settings—remain in the arena and emerge victorious at the end of their marathon? How do some ministers manage to run the race and "finish strong" while so many others drop
out, becoming casualties of the ministerial minefield?

As we explore questions like these while interviewing pastors
and leaders around the globe, several clear patterns emerge from the
lifestyles, choices, and perspectives of the healthy survivors. Those
who endure and thrive seem to share some common traits that run

deeper than mere personality or temperament type. Rather than being equipped by nature to handle stress successfully, those who endure hardship and emerge victorious seem to have determined their course by force of will. They have made some decisions about their mind-set and their priorities, and those decisions appear to have a quantifiable impact on later outcomes.

So what are these key decisions and choices?

What do healthy survivors of ministerial struggles appear to share in common despite differences in age, race, culture, context, and experience?

We'll look at these common traits in this chapter.

Secret No. 1: A Core Mind-set that Is Focused on Eternity

Life on this earth will always be stressful.

We are not guaranteed a stress-free environment until we reach heaven. Until then—for as long as we are alive on this earth—we can and should expect stressful situations to emerge and occur. Stress is a normal consequence of being alive in a fallen world. Stress is a natural byproduct of sharing this spinning planet with a few billion other human beings—people whose values, priorities, and attitudes may be in conflict with our own.

Pastors who are healthy and thriving seem to know this by heart.

Here and now: life on this earth will always be stressful.

Christ himself mentioned this salient fact to his disciples, just in case their own expectations were out of touch with reality. Christ may have feared that his followers might think of discipleship as being some kind of free pass—escaping the troubles and tribulations of this world due to their close connection with God or their committed following of his Son. So, does becoming more spiritual mean that we are unaffected by the hassles of the world around us, safe in our own cocoon?

Healthy ministers know better. They expect relief from struggle in the next life rather than looking for it during this brief sojourn on earth. Hear and learn: life on this earth will always be stressful.

Christ makes this truth abundantly clear. "In this world you will have trouble," Jesus says (John 16:33) in what may be a radical understatement of our context and experience as Christians. Yet before leaving us with that thought and its impact, Christ goes on to mention a modifying aspect of the trouble we will face.

"But take heart! I have overcome the world."

We need to hear these two truths, and we need to hear them in exactly this chronological order. First, we should expect to face stress in the world—or if you prefer, we should anticipate much "trouble." We need to believe this, expect this, and regard this truth as our normative experience. Christ was no stranger to trouble—he was often in conflict with church authorities, often slandered and opposed, and finally crucified by secular authorities to whom he had prescribed allegiance and faithfulness in all due obligations. He honored them; they crucified him.

Fairness and justice?

Not exactly features of Christ's life on this earth.

So as someone who knew stress and experienced it daily, Jesus accurately tells his followers that they, too, should expect to encounter turbulence and difficulty as they go about their journeys and follow him. Trouble is normative here. Stress is a given in this life. Anyone who tells you differently is selling something.

Once we realize and accept that stress is normal, Christ does not leave us there. He goes on to explain a second and parallel truth that we also need to know: "Take heart! I have overcome the world." So although this world will be the setting of our stress—often and normally—it is also true that this troubled world has already been overcome by a higher power. The stress of this earth is not the final answer. It does not have final authority over us.

Our stress on earth endures for a season, just as we do—we flourish like the grass of the field and then we are gone. In the same way, the troubles and stresses of this life will endure for a season—but they do not have the power to mark us for eternity because they have already been defeated and overcome.

The final scoreboard looks like this: Christ 1, world 0.

So while we wait for the stress-free eternity that lies ahead, what should console and encourage us? Where should we find our strength to endure?

Paul addresses this question while writing to the church at Rome. Paul, himself no stranger to encounters with difficulty and opposition, tells the Romans that nothing can separate us from the love of Christ (see Romans 8:35-39) and then goes on to list a wide range of troubles, trials, tribulations, difficulties—sources of stress that may seem overwhelming and impossible.

Yet these daunting circumstances are no match for the love of God, Paul reminds us. It is the love of God that holds us, keeps us, secures our future, and enables us to endure our present. While we experience these diverse troubles—and we will—we are actively and passionately being held close in the love of God, kept safe for an enduring season that will follow. In our eternal destination with God, these trivial troubles will no longer be present.

Paul is clear about this.

He writes, "I consider that our present sufferings are not worth comparing with the glory that will be revealed in us" (Romans 8:18). We should expect to suffer in this world, especially if we follow Christ. Yet these sufferings that seem so large and difficult now are not remotely comparable to the magnitude and impact of the glory that God is holding for us in eternity.

Pastors who thrive have fixed these two truths in their minds.

They know that life on earth will be stressful, and they regard this as normal.

They also know that in the bigger picture—from the mind-set of eternity—these troubles are trifles. They are no match for God's love; they will not endure for one moment longer than God permits or allows. The day is coming, and perhaps it is coming soon, when God will say "no more" and the troubles of this life will end.

Pastors who thrive have a core mind-set that is focused on eternity. They know and expect that their true rewards are kept safe for them in heaven. They know and expect that life on earth will involve battles, setbacks, superficial and also deep wounds, and ongoing adversity. They also know that the love of God can and does hold them safe through these things, and that heaven is coming soon.

Secret No. 2: A Core Passion for Intimacy with God

Here is a useful prescription for avoiding burnout in ministry: focus your attention on drawing closer to God, becoming intimate with him. Set your sights on a deeper walk, a fuller knowledge, and a stronger friendship with God himself—then follow where he leads you on a daily basis.

Too often we who minister are tempted to substitute deeds performed in the name of God—or acts of service done on behalf of God—for what is really needed: a deep and personal relationship with God. Too often we who minister are inclined to functionally live as though we have to earn our way into God's good graces, appearing to believe that if we don't perform well, we will be shut out of God's favor. We become productive and busy pastors—serving and acting, coming and going, achieving and doing—while missing the mark.

We substitute the practice for the presence.

While we claim to be busy doing what matters, we are actually ignoring what matters the most. In the midst of our ministerial busyness and achievements, we may be putting our very souls in jeopardy. We have misdirected our focus. We are doing instead of being, acting instead of dwelling, anxious instead of composed.

Here is a question that is well worth considering: How many times will God lead us into burnout?

How often will God guide us toward overpromising, overfunctioning, overcommitting, or overperforming? Is this God's pattern for us: overdoing?

We live in the hurry and the worry, and we minister from our own poverty.

Unwittingly, perhaps, we begin to draw ministry from our own strength, and the natural outcome of this behavior is both sad and also quite predictable. When we minister from our own strength, we are always drawing upon a finite source and a dwindling supply. Our own resources are limited and easily depleted. We are like a canteen that splashes broadly and empties out its contents quickly, when God's purpose is that we should be wells of water, ever-springing, living and ministering from the overflow of our own deep relationship with him.

Those who thrive in ministry tend to understand this truth, not merely as an intellectual idea but rather as a prescribed pattern for living. They know that if they seek God, follow God, and desire God with all their hearts, God will lead them wisely and well. They know that God will not put them on the path to destruction. They choose to let God lead, allowing him to set both the direction and the pace.

So where and how will God lead us, if we seek him above all else?

"He leads me beside quiet waters, he refreshes my soul," proclaims the Psalmist (Psalm 23:2). This is the polar opposite of ministerial overload and pastoral burnout. This is the therapeutic and ongoing antidote for the toxins of ministerial stress. This is a picture of a life that is focused on letting our shepherd lead, seeking fellowship and friendship with our shepherd as we follow him.

And while God is leading us beside still waters, he also restores our soul. When we minister from a restored soul, we serve others from our possession of abundance rather than from our position of authority. We allow ourselves to decrease, so that God's presence in us can increase.

When we are walking beside those still waters, we have an inner peace that transcends and exceeds the external traumas all around us. We are participating with God in our own healing as a proactive lifestyle. We are daily being restored by the presence of God and his Holy Spirit in us.

Those who thrive in ministry understand this with their very lives.

They are not trying to teach others a precept or a principle so that their minds can grasp it. Instead, they are focused on a core passion of drawing closer to God, letting God set the parameters and boundaries of their ministerial motions. God can add or subtract, accelerate or slow things down, change their careers, or reestablish his intention that they serve in their present places. All of these issues and more are fixed firmly in a relationship with the Father that supersedes all else.

Lest we miss the importance of this, Christ reminds us of this truth during his brief tenure here on earth. Christ points out the obvious: God's design is not aimed at our destruction, but instead on our renewal and health.

"Take my yoke upon you and learn of me," Christ advises (Matthew 11:29). Lest we see this as yet another burden to lift, Christ continues his instruction set. "For my yoke is easy and my burden is light" (Matthew 11:30).

An easy yoke?

A light burden?

This is not how a busy, multitasking pastor is likely to describe his or her ministry. Instead, we may hear how busy he is right now, how many roles she fulfills in the church, or how much programming and activity is going on in the broader community of faith.

If we listen with careful ears, we might hear this as a sign that a core passion may be missing from the minister. We may be encountering someone who is missing the mark, trading a flurry of activity for the flavors of renewal.

God leads us beside still waters, restoring our souls.

Christ's yoke is easy; his burden is light.

These are deep truths that stress-resistant pastors know by experience. They are like trees planted by the watercourse, bringing forth fruit in their season (see Psalm 1:3). These ministers are saturated with an innate generosity of spirit that is not of their own making; it is an inheritance of the life that follows God's design.

John Piper is accurate and correct when he points us to "desiring God." When this desire is highest among our competing affections, we are focused in the right direction. The leadership of our lives is in good hands: his. We can be sure of his care and his tending of our deepest needs.

Secret No. 3: A Core Priority for a Quality Marriage

"My husband has a mistress," the pastor's wife confided in us as we gathered for a counseling session at a church conference, "and it's not another woman; it's the church. He has time for everything and everyone in the congregation, no matter what they ask and no matter when they call. I feel like his passion and his energy are always being given away—but not to me. When he comes in the door at night, he is exhausted and worn out, unable or unwilling to engage me in conversation or relationship or intimacy. And before any of that could begin anyway, the phone rings and he's gone again, out the door caring for someone else."

This wife speaks for many; her lament is a well-established complaint.

Yet somehow pastors who thrive in ministry have learned to make their marriage a high priority—higher than always being available, higher than growing the church to a larger size, higher than the non-stop ministry of "being there" that takes so many pastors away from their partners night after night, time after time.

The stress-resistant pastor knows a secret: make the marriage a key focus, valuing the spouse above the conflicting demands and competing priorities of life in pastoral ministry. When a life partner understands that he or she comes first, and the needs of ministry are farther down the priority list, a relationship thrives and a marriage improves.

The fruit of this is a healthier minister and a happier mate.

We speak at Ministers and Mates Retreats across North America and beyond. Anecdotally, we are observing that more and more ministers understand the need to value a spouse above a job, a relationship above a career. The old idea that somehow serving the church was more spiritual than making a marriage work may be passing away into obscurity. If so, it cannot possibly perish quickly enough.

Those who serve in ministry are often indeed "on call" for emergency and crisis situations. In a smaller church, it may seem that the crisis network is fairly limited: one person, the pastor, handles almost everything. This mind-set that every emergency requires the pastor's attention and that every need is the pastor's responsibility should be addressed by another book in another time. For now, it's enough to note that building the marriage relationship is more important than fixing the furnace, attending yet another meeting, or leading the workday or mission trip.

Larger church pastors understand this and tend to live it. They develop systems and networks that respond to emergencies and that carry the load of primary pastoral care—hospital visits, prayers for the sick, and responding to many kinds of trauma and disaster. While the lead or senior pastor is free to participate in these kinds of events, it is not the expectation that he or she will do so. Instead, the small-group members or the Stephen's ministers or the men and women on the pastoral care team are considered "first responders" when a need arises.

Smaller church pastors may feel like they carry the weight of the world on their shoulders; because of this belief, they are accordingly more likely to leave a spouse feeling abandoned or unloved. It is here in the arena of smaller-church ministry that we encounter so many spouses who wish that their partners were not pastors. Some of them state this wish explicitly and often; others express it from a wide range of collateral observation points.

Dr. Woodie Stevens serves the global Church of the Nazarene as the director of Sunday School and Discipleship Ministries International. A busy and popular conference and retreat speaker, Dr. Stevens has also served as a DS and in other key roles of denominational leadership. In reflecting on the connections between marital health and pastoral ministry, Stevens observes that "the health of the marriage relationship within the parsonage family has an enormous impact on the effectiveness of pastoral ministry."[1]

In other words, it is difficult to establish and maintain an effective pastoral presence if one's own marriage is in disarray. While it may be possible to fool some of the people some of the time, sooner or later marital health or the lack of it tends to be visible to those in the larger community. A pastor who cannot or will not make his or her own marriage a high priority will inevitably lose respect among the very people he or she is trying to lead.

The mantra "Watch what I say; ignore what I do" may fall on deaf ears.

By contrast, a pastor whose own marriage is thriving and healthy (not perfect, but visibly thriving) derives relational authority and life authority from the context of living marriage well. When God is visible in a marriage relationship, and when it is clear to all that the pastor values and cherishes his or her life partner, the foundations of powerful family ministry are set in place. Now the church is being led not by expounding good ideas and principles but rather by modeling good practice.

This good practice—regardless of its peripheral impact on the congregation—brings its own rewards in the pastor's private life at home. A satisfied spouse tends to create an environment in the home that renews and encourages the busy minister. No longer does the pastor dread going home, wondering what kind of mood or attitude he or she may encounter. No longer does the minister plan yet another meeting as a way of escaping the negative or perhaps overtly hostile environment in the parsonage.

When the spouse's position and priority is clearly established and visibly honored, the other valid priorities of ministry can find their proper place. There will always be other priorities, but when these are set below the level of deepening and growing the pastor's marriage, relational health can thrive.

Stress-resistant pastors understand and practice this truth. They make their spouse a priority; they also tend to verbalize this priority within their context. They make explicit to the leaders and the congregation what is already evident privately: that building the marriage and honoring the spouse will be the pastor's highest priority after serving God. Congregational matters are important and will find their place, but their place is somewhat down the ladder from the spouse's high position of honor, value, and respect.

Churches who fail to understand the wisdom of this perspective may not deserve having a pastor to care for them. As with whiny children, their manipulative and unhelpful selfishness might best be ignored. A church that wants to have first place in their pastor's heart may be fundamentally unsound and spiritually unsafe and should perhaps be left to its own devices and beliefs. There is no reason to sacrifice a pastor's marriage on the altar of misguided priorities.

Secret No. 4: A Core Focus on the Family

Stress-resistant pastors raise healthy kids in loving homes.

They do so without stressing the "fishbowl" nature of life in the parsonage. They do so without insisting that their children and teens serve as "models" for others to follow. They accept the pressures and burdens of pastoral ministry yet choose to spare their children the weight of undue or unrealistic expectations.

They know how to raise great kids—by loving them, believing in them, and granting them generous measures of quality time.

Across two decades of serving as speakers and resource persons at retreats for teen PKs and MKs (adolescents who are the children of pastors, missionaries, and other church leaders), we can tell when a pastor or minister makes his family a high priority in his daily life. His children are well-adjusted and social; they tend to have huge hearts for others and may even sense a call toward future ministry.

They do not regard ministry as a dead-end street or a vocation of last resort. They tend to see ministry as a wonderful way to help people. They tend to see those who minister as altruistic, well-motivated, bright, and capable. In other words they often want to grow up to be just like their parents!

We worked with some of the best and brightest of these well-adjusted teens in the state of Minnesota, across an arc of many seasons. We returned in several consecutive years to speak and counsel at a retreat for the teen PKs and MKs of this state, learning to love and value each member of this cohort. Each year the retreat was held in the picture-perfect setting of Big Sandy Camp (CMA) along the shores of Big Sandy Lake in McGregor, Minnesota.

One thing we quickly realized about this diverse group: the majority felt cherished and loved by their parents. It was clear that the ministers of this region were doing a great job of focusing on their families; we could quantify and measure their success one smiling face at a time. Busy serving pastorates in large metro areas and in small rural communities, these pastors and spouses were raising well-adjusted, others-focused teens with big hearts for God and his kingdom.

Year after year, we would travel to serve and minister to this great group, yet end up receiving a lot of powerful ministry while we served. We came to counsel and lead, to speak and advise, to pray and to mentor. Yet year after year and retreat after retreat we also received wise counsel, heard wise things being said, and were prayed for by high school or middle school teens who had huge hearts for ministry. There was a blur between the giving and the receiving as we learned, appreciated, grew, stretched, and were impacted by the prayers and the love of the members of this group.

These bright people know who they are: across the years we have attended their graduations from high school and college, joyously performed their weddings, and gladly participated in the dedications of their children. To this day, the members of this particular cohort have a special place in our hearts. And more broadly, their parents also have a place in our hearts because of the highly effective way that they made their families a priority while also serving in challenging places of ministry.

Although we travel widely and make friends easily, the teen PKs and MKs of this state have remained printed on our hearts at a deep level. They call us Mom and Dad without displacing the high-quality people who have earned those titles. We call them our children—a declaration of affection, parental pride, and much joy.

As we got to know the parents of these teens, we saw quality marriages, a high investment in family time, a heart for God and a passion for knowing him, and the virtue of serving others while maintaining good personal boundaries. Any of these parents could author this section of our book; they've earned the right.

When you make your family a priority, it shows in the results.

Secret No. 5: An Effort to Create Financial Margin

Dr. Gerard Reed, who taught and lectured at two Christian universities, explained the nature of true wealth to several generations of students as they enrolled in his history classes or courses in philosophy.

There are only two ways to become wealthy, Reed would argue. One can either have more or want less. Passionately and with the gifts and graces of a great teacher, Reed would argue in favor of the latter option. He would endorse what M. Scott Peck calls "the road less traveled" and would point his students in the direction of downward mobility—a clarion call in a culture that values materialism, consumption, and conspicuous excess.

Generation after generation of students heeded the call, many of them choosing occupations in missions or ministry—places where the path to wealth would not involve acquiring more, but would instead involve "wanting less."

Stress-resistant pastors are actively engaged in the process of creating financial margins for themselves and their families. They do so in a wide range of ways and using their varied gifts; there is no "one size fits all" approach to this particular stress-busting pursuit. Yet as we survey the landscape of healthy, stress-resistant pastors, there is a clear trend indicating the value of financial margin as it creates emotional "space" for the pastoral family.

Rev. Raymond Bridges served churches across the southeastern USA, often accepting assignments of challenged or troubled churches. He was an early pioneer of the so-called church doctor model—where a wise, experienced pastor is sent to an unhealthy environment in order to lead and facilitate effective change.

In church after church, in setting after setting, Bridges infused previously unhealthy congregations with his own infectious brand of holy optimism. He had a natural energy and enthusiasm that the

Gallup Strength Finders would label "woo." After spending even a few minutes in his presence one tended to feel better, be encouraged, and to believe that a bright future was possible.

Rev. Bridges shared these character and personality traits with his wife, Nan. Both Ray and Nan Bridges had smiles that lit up a room and had character that raised up godly generations where previously only dysfunction and ill health had reigned. These two gifted servants were turnaround specialists who never served what we now call a megachurch but whose gifts for ministry were exceptional.

As they ministered and served, accepting dubious assignments with low or minimal pay, both Ray and Nan believed in the virtue of creating financial margin. Across the years they engaged in a wide range of businesses that provided income and support for their family. This outside income gave them considerable freedom in dealing with stubborn or change-resistant churches. Because they raised support from their own labors outside the congregation, they were never at the mercy of a capricious church treasurer or a miserly church board.

Their emotional lives were well served by the existence of financial margin. Their homes—and they built, maintained, and established many fine homes—were places of joy and refuge, sanctuary and sanity. It was always a blessing to be entertained by these two— especially within the walls of their home. Their laughter, wisdom, courage, and courtesy were legendary.

Having financial margin gave them the freedom to minister without currying favor, attempting to please people, or bending the truth of the gospel to fit ears that resisted hearing it. They could serve as Jesus served, lead as Jesus led—and if the results weren't spectacular, their own family was well cared for by the efforts they made in secular businesses.

The pastor of a struggling church in the Midwest decided to follow this example during a dry spell in his own ministry. After serving the congregation for several years, he felt personally stagnant and perceived his ministry as being less effective than he hoped. Additionally, the church was not growing, and the financial resources of the church did not support the pastor's family in an acceptable way.

As he prayed for a way forward, this pastor believes that God guided his steps toward a secular employer in the community. He accepted a part-time role at a big box retailer in the area, earning a decent hourly wage for the hours that he could offer. Within weeks his family was expressing gratitude for the privileges and blessings that the new, extra income provided. Meanwhile, the secular setting gave this deeply committed minister a brand-new arena in which to witness and counsel.

"I think I may be a more effective pastor at [secular employer] than I am in my own congregation," this pastor remarked over coffee. "I have engaged in more conversations about Christ, I have found more spiritual readiness, and I have already watched several accept Christ and begin attending church. I am almost at the point where I am doing more ministry outside the church than inside it."

Over a period of several years this outside employment began to have a positive impact on the congregation, as new believers were added to the Kingdom. As this happened in the congregation there was also a happier, more relaxed parsonage family because the pastor's second job was providing more income, allowing the family to go places and do things that had never been possible before.

Let's be crystal clear about the scale of this, financially. No one was becoming rich. The pastor didn't lease a Mercedes or begin wearing $5,000 suits. Instead, the existence of steady part-time work began to provide financial margin for the pastor and his family, which in turn created emotional margin within the home.

Here is a new twist on bivocational complexity. There may be times when a second job is not a detriment to ministry but instead enables the pastor to enjoy ministry in a new way. Now—depending on the outside job and its pay level—the pastor and his family may experience some new freedoms and welcome privileges that were never possible on the income that the church alone provided.

Whether by scaling back, reducing our wishes, or by acquiring a source of additional income, the creation of financial margin is a healthy habit that is known and valued by stress-resistant pastors. Although they merit their church salaries and are probably worth more than the church provides, these pastors enjoy a sense of stress-reducing emotional margin that is made possible by the additional financial resources.

For Ray and Nan Bridges, it was a paper route, a vending machine company, or private music lessons, among other ventures. Place by place and city by city they looked for ways to supplement their income, not by accepting charity, but by working to earn a living from outside sources. Within days of arriving in a new setting they would be building a network or a business, establishing a presence in the larger community, and planning their pathway toward financial margin.

They were vibrantly healthy in spiritual ways—and they needed to be as they accepted calls to dysfunctional, troubled, or deeply conflicted congregations. As their infectious good health infected the congregations they served, these two found ways to create financial margin by being industrious, creative, and smart.

Their intentional creation of financial margin is a wise and virtuous trait shared by stress-resistant pastors on several continents and in widely varying cultures and settings. Although the cost of living varies widely among these diverse settings, the unifying theme is that margin for living must be created by intentional and strategic design—with God's help. Financial margin, like other types of margin in your life, does not create itself.

If you want to enjoy financial margin, your choices are exactly those framed by Dr. Gerard Reed in his many classes: either have more or want less. Making progress in both areas at the same time is the fastest way forward.

In and among these five secrets are tips and traditions that can help you make the journey toward stress-resistance and wholeness. By adopting one or more of these strategies, you may find the ability not just to endure stress and survive its effects but to actually over-come stress and thrive in your current setting of ministry.

That—succinctly stated—is the purpose of this chapter and also the underlying purpose of this book. Since stress will always be with us, the goal is to develop core values, core beliefs, and core habits that transform your reality from stressed-out to stress-resistant, allowing you to literally "have a life."

9
COPING MECHANISMS: FOUR HABITS THAT CAN LOWER YOUR STRESS

In the previous chapter, we looked at five secrets of stress-resistant pastors. These secrets were rooted in priorities and values, in choices and decisions, in perspectives and understandings. Although they can and should apply immediately to life, they are rooted in the mind-set of a pastor and the mental processes by which a pastor makes decisions about his or her priorities in ministry.

In this chapter, we'll take a simpler approach, looking at practical habits that a pastor might employ in order to accomplish goals like increasing financial margin, developing quality connections with a spouse, or improving a family's sense of unity and togetherness. Where in the previous chapter we were looking at a largely theoretical framework, in this chapter we will do some basic nuts and bolts of looking at practical habits for lowering your stress.

We call these coping mechanisms because they have the effect of lowering your stress, increasing your quality of life, giving you an emotional or spiritual lift, and improving your attitudes—as well as those of your partner and children. These four habits are distilled from more than two decades of learning from pastors and their spouses, from pastors' children and their unvarnished, straight-as-nails reports about what it feels like to grow up in a parsonage.

By adopting one or more of these practical habits, you can enable your partner and family to better appreciate life and ministry—because, if you adopt even one of these strategies, you will be well on the road to "having a life."

Without further introduction, here are four helpful habits for lowering the stress in your pastoral home.

Create an FMZ: Family Meal Zone

The family meal zone is a brand-new concept based on a centuries-old tradition of gathering together for meals as a family. Remember that? Maybe if you're now in your grandparenting years. If you're younger than that, you may have few actual memories of a family gathered around a meal table together. The rare exceptions might be major holidays—but even then, your family probably divided into groups and sections, with some watching football, some grabbing food and running upstairs, some standing around the kitchen eating and talking, and so on.

The core concept of an FMZ does not involve that kind of fractured family time but instead unifies a family around a common table, a common meal, and a tradition of talking and listening, sharing and learning, and staying in touch with each other's feelings.

Yes, your family could simply scan each other's Facebook pages while on the run to the next soccer game. You're doing that now, right? So as a popular television psychologist might ask: "How's that working out for you?"

A family meal zone is an intentional, deliberate period of time during which each member of the family disconnects from Internet, telecommunications, any device with a screen, any game or distraction, and actually makes eye contact with other members of the family around the table.

We realize the completely radical nature of this unusual suggestion. The idea is that a family develops a habit of doing this, perhaps starting with one meal a week. Perhaps also, for the sake of consistency, it is always the same meal during the week—say (choosing at random) a Tuesday night meal.

If you decide to attempt this strategy, you will quickly discover that the entire world conspires to distract, dissuade, and change your plans so that Tuesday is not possible for a family gathering. And the same is true if you pick Friday, or Sunday, or any other day of the week. No matter what you attempt, the schedules and priorities of each member of your family will definitely conflict with your efforts—and probably sooner rather than later.

Be determined and confident.

Stick to your plans.

Once you've decided to attempt a family meal zone, be resolute in your efforts to make it happen. And—especially if you are a parent—model the kinds of behaviors you are trying to produce in your children. Turn off the TV in the other room, even though you're not really watching it. Shut it off anyway; make it clear that this period of time (thirty to ninety minutes) is completely for and about being together as a family.

If you've never tried having family devotions together, you might add that concept into this one. Otherwise, you're trying to build two new habits, and you're trying to get two things on the schedule. Since you're already making a powerful effort to bring everyone together for a common meal, consider having a prayer together or reading a Bible verse together as one feature of your own FMZ.

Recent studies confirm what previous studies have always concluded: being together at mealtime helps a family be unified and gives children and teens a sense of security and well-being that might otherwise be absent.

A recent study reported in the *Journal of Adolescent Health* concluded that the more frequently teens (ages eleven through fifteen in this study) ate meals with their families, the fewer emotional and mental problems they experienced. The study was based on a broad 26,000-youth sample of Canadian adolescents, yet the findings are consistent with other studies in previous eras and different settings.[1]

Whether the studies look at children or adolescents, persons or families, the results point consistently toward the conclusion that simple family togetherness around a meal yields tangible benefits in mental and emotional health. These benefits are the most pronounced for adolescents and teens, yet adults are also the beneficiaries of family bonding around the meal table.

If you decide to establish a family meal zone, and if you choose to have a consistent pattern for this—for example, every Tuesday night—you may be wise to tell friends, extended family, and even your church leaders that for a block of time each Tuesday night you will be out of communication. You will not be responding to phone calls, text messages, emails, or any other form of contact. You should let them know that you are not monitoring these devices during this period of time.

Here is how one minister's wife reported on her family's success with this particular strategy, after going through the difficult process of first establishing and then enforcing a family meal zone.

Her conclusions:

"Watching Allen play with our two small children during one of our early FMZ times, I fell in love with him all over again. He's so great with the kids! Watching him down on his knees playing with them, I realized what a great dad he is and how blessed I am that he is my husband.

"Who knew that watching my husband play with our kids could be so romantic and so encouraging? It really changed the way I see him."

This wife's report is similar in nature and tone to the comments we receive from other men and women who make the decision to set up an FMZ for their own parsonage families. Almost all of them report that it takes effort, that it doesn't come together simply or easily, and that they may have to try several different meals or times before they find one that consistently works. But having said that, they also consistently tell us that the FMZ is making a positive difference for their families.

Although some of these ministers and mates may have had the idea or concept of "eat more meals together," somehow it actually starts to happen when they declare it a "family meal zone" and begin to implement this as a strategy. Somewhere in this process, something that was a dream or an idea becomes a tangible reality that is positively impacting the daily life and emotional health of the family.

Outsourcing: It's Not Just for Giant Corporations

One of the more challenging aspects of pastoring a smaller church is that there is not a large team of staff members carrying out the wide range of duties that are needed to help a church run smoothly.

Sometimes a pastor looks in the mirror in the morning, perhaps while shaving, and catches a glimpse of the entire team.

Need a furnace fixed? You're looking at the team member.

Copy machine broke down again? You're looking at the repair person.

Somehow the pastors of smaller churches are often the ones who get the call when a problem emerges with the church's physical plant, office equipment, or premises. So while the pastor is already running in all directions doing the care of members and families, the same pastor is also expected to take care of a myriad of details of church life, some of them absolutely mundane and trivial.

Hence the habit: outsourcing.

Larger churches have secretaries, staff members, leaders of volunteer teams, and much more. In a smaller church, you may have only yourself. What's needed is a paradigm shift: instead of seeing the church janitor in the mirror, try seeing the coordinator of church volunteer services.

Let's face it: Are you a born copy machine repair person? If so, by all means enjoy and deploy your useful talents. But if not, it may be time to help someone in your church rise up and take care of maintaining the office equipment. The same advice applies to the church restrooms, the church parking lot, the church lawn, and every other feature of church life that does not fit within your "calling" as a minister. Remember when you thought you were pursuing a *spiritual* career?

Outsourcing: it happens all the time in large corporations.

Previous generations might have called this delegating.

Welcome to the twenty-first century. In this generation, we use the term *outsourcing* to describe a process by which various jobs, duties, and roles are given to outside contractors, freeing up the corporation's employees and executives for more relevant assignments. If a giant multinational corporation can figure out how to do this, so can you.

Consider outsourcing the lawn care, bathroom cleaning, office machine repair, errands to restock church supplies, kitchen cleaning, or whatever stray duties you believe are "expected of you" as the pastor. You may discover that you have retired persons, stay-at-home spouses, or others who not only can take over these duties but also will enjoy feeling like they are making a contribution.

That feeling is also a reality: by taking up these peripheral roles, such persons are making a contribution toward lower stress in the pastoral family and more quality time between pastor and spouse and pastor and children.

That contribution is absolutely real, not imaginary.

The Famous "Four-Dollar Banquet"

Across North America and around the globe, we have shared an idea from our own relationship that we affectionately call the four-dollar banquet. Although adjusted for local currencies and specific costs of living, the small dollar amount is still a current figure for our North American conference and seminar attendees.

Participate in any marriage renewal event, marriage retreat, or conference aimed at better marriages, and someone will tell you to have a date night. Someone may guilt you into believing that unless you and your spouse have a date night, you won't be getting closer together as a couple. Generation after generation of marriage presenters and marriage educators continue to expound on this idea of a date night, telling thousands of couples that the pathway to bliss runs through this particular neighborhood and concept.

We choose to disagree, as follows.

You don't have to go on a date.

It doesn't have to be at night.

Simple enough? What matters is that the two of you make some time to be together, time to simply enjoy each other's company. This is not problem-solving time or strategic planning time (though those may be useful ideas too). This is time to just enjoy being together—relaxed, unstressed, unhurried time together as just you two.

We call our version the four-dollar banquet, and that's a pretty close price quote.

Here's how it works: we go to a Starbucks or a Panera Bread or a Caribou Coffee or that great little independent venue in your city or town. Chances are, even in the remote wilderness where you live, someone runs a small coffee shop.

So you start there. It isn't a date, and you don't have to go at night. You simply make your way to that coffee shop together, setting aside an hour or two of time that you will just be together as a couple.

Find a booth in the corner.

Ignore, as much as possible, everyone else in the room. This is usually not too challenging—they're all busy updating their Facebook pages, accessing the free Wi-Fi on their iPhones or tablets. See? They don't even know you exist.

How we keep our expenses to $4 is this: we purchase one coffee, and the other partner just has a water (not bottled, not French, not special), which is usually free of charge. In fact, many coffee shops have pitchers of ice water already set out for the use of the customers. Barnes and Noble Bookstores feature this kind of ice water available in their in-store coffee areas.

So we purchase one coffee, then we also buy two cookies or two sliced muffin tops (a Panera item but available elsewhere), which usually ranges from about $0.99 to $1.29 per cookie or muffin top. The total bill—one coffee, two cookies—consistently comes to about four dollars. Since you are ordering at a counter and taking your drink to your own table, there is no server to tip.

This is a controlled-expense environment. No waitress. No menu. No expensive meals followed by expensive desserts. No over-priced beverages, unless you prefer your coffee whooshed through a steam machine and injected with various foreign flavors. If so, help yourself, but you just blew the entire four dollars on the beverage, and you don't have a cookie yet.

You noticed that, right?

We are thrifty.

Or perhaps you might say, cheap.

The point is, our own version of the ubiquitous "date night" is not expensive. It is almost ridiculously cheap. We do not consider it a date, and it does not usually happen at night. We like the mid-morning gap between breakfast and lunch or the midafternoon but before-school-is-out gap. We love those particular time frames, but your schedules and preferences may vary. Suit yourselves! That's the whole point.

Frankly, the atmosphere in the corner of the coffee shop, while everyone else chatters away or plays with their small screens, can often be quite conducive to cozy conversation and emotional intimacy with your partner. The two of you can be "all alone" in the midst of coffee shop chaos.

We've been doing this for more than a decade, and it works—simply and well.

If you don't like coffee, you have it even better. Order two waters and you can overachieve on the financial front. You'll be enjoying a two-dollar banquet and receiving the same benefits we do, except for the warm caffeine.

"Home Alone 2": Not the Movie

Our fourth and final suggestion is also quite cheap—or in other words, it is entirely in character for us. We love finding ways to connect relationally without draining the bank financially.

This one is called home alone 2, and that is exactly the point.

Find an afternoon or an evening when you can farm out the kids. If they are already in school at a set time every day, and if your two schedules as adults permit and allow this—try home alone 2 during schooltime. In this way, you have already avoided the potential expense of a sitter.

If you're working with an evening, you may have a teen in your church or in your neighborhood who will watch your kids for a reasonable fee. Your goal is to drop the kids at that person's home or to have that person take your kids to a safe location for a while. Meanwhile, you'll have your house all to yourselves.

If there are other couples in your church who also have children, you can use the barter exchange idea, swapping child care among families. You watch theirs, they watch yours, and everyone benefits. In this way, you avoid the cost of a sitter again, because families take turns bearing the shared responsibility. So no one pays someone to watch the children—instead, each family helps out in turn.

You may have parents, siblings, relatives, close friends, or others who will also watch your children without charge. Grandparents may be glad to be available, and they are certainly not expecting to be paid! In fact, they may spend their time spoiling your kids at McDonald's or Walmart—yet another bonus overall.

Meanwhile your goal is to be home alone. Someone reliable and trustworthy is watching the kids, and you two are home as adults without your usual duties as parents.

This is not the time to clean the house—although it's a noble idea.

This is not the time to solve all your relational problems; save that for a nice long drive to visit the distant relatives. You'll be trapped in the car anyway, and if the kids are along you'll be more cordial, more polite, and less likely to say things that you'll later regret.

So—you are not in house-cleaning or problem-solving mode.

This is time to be together as two. It can be or become a sexual highlight of your week, but it needn't have that pressure or expectation attached to it. You can rent a one-dollar movie from the Redbox, order a delivery pizza, or cook a frozen one right there in your own microwave. You can fall asleep on the couch, cuddled together as two, and not have sexual expectations attached to that.

At the core of home alone 2 is a simple idea. You are not out spending money somewhere on a fancy dinner or an overpriced movie. Have you priced a first-run movie ticket during the evening hours? Have you priced two tickets? The core of this idea is stay home and don't spend much money.

Redbox.

Pizza.

Cheap.

Make your own entertainment if you prefer.

Be lazy and carefree.

We've had couples attempt a home alone 2 and tell us later that they both noshed on chips and salsa (all they could afford) and then fell asleep on the couch.

As if that's a bad outcome? Whoa—not even slightly. The two of you relaxed and dining together, cuddling together on the sofa—you've got a license, so it's entirely and completely okay if you sleep together.

Building a habit of occasional home alone 2 times will help you get into a pattern of relaxing together, enjoying each other, and being away from kids and other distractions (we mean, priorities). Couples who make this effort soon find that both husband and wife look forward to home alone 2 and enjoy making it a regular part of their schedule. You may make the same discovery!

To sum up, we often make marriage enrichment more complicated and more expensive than it really needs to be. Of course, your marriage might improve if the two of you ran off to Maui for a week and didn't take the kids. But let's get real. About how often is that going to happen in the real world? That's why the ideas in this chapter are aimed at affordability, simplicity, and accessibility.

Of course, miracles do happen.

Somewhere along the journey of ministry, you may actually encounter a board member or parishioner who owns a time-share and wants to be generous with it, allowing the pastor some privileges. Some nice person may actually offer you a week in a clean, attractive condo somewhere, with or without your kids.

Given an offer like that, wouldn't you find a way to make that happen? Of course you would.

Meanwhile, in the real world of limited finances, emotional exhaustion, the stress of parenting, and the stress of ministry, you can learn how to take small steps in positive directions. Maybe a four-dollar banquet is just the right ticket for you. Or maybe a home alone 2 is exactly what the doctor ordered!

Happy pastoral families and fulfilled clergy couples receive their own reward, but as counselors we actually believe that good health produces more good health. Modeling a healthy marriage and a positive family life in your ministry will most likely lead to healthier marriages in your congregation and happier families among your community. People will learn from your example as much as, or perhaps more than, they learn from your sermons.

Let your life speak by showing people that you value, cherish, and respect your life partner. Let your example speak by demonstrating that you value your children and you are enforcing a family meal zone just to be with them.

In these small and simple ways, you will be leading others whether or not you know it. And rather than giving them an example that is too expensive or too complex to follow, you will be modeling some highly reproducible ideas.

We call these habits stress-reducing because couple after couple, minister after minister, family after family has reported back with positive results. These are pastor-tested, pastor-approved ideas for reducing your emotional stress.

Try one or try them all.

Use them exactly as suggested here or modify them to fit your own time, temperaments, and preferences.

But one way or another—get into some new habits.

Get out there and lead—try a four-dollar banquet this week!

ABOUT THE AUTHORS

Dr. David and Lisa Frisbie

Dr. David and Lisa Frisbie jointly serve as executive directors of the Center for Marriage and Family Studies in Del Mar, California. Although they engage across a broad spectrum of family topics, they have invested much attention regarding the topics of clergy marriages, military marriages, and remarriages/blended families. Since the late 1980s, they have often been referred to as America's remarriage experts due to their extensive array of publications and speaking on this topic.

Dr. and Mrs. Frisbie are the authors or coauthors of twenty-five books about issues in family life. Among their more recent titles published by Beacon Hill Press are *Dating after Divorce: Preparing for a New Relationship* (2012) and a two-book set for premarital counseling, *Right from the Start: A Premarital Guide for Couples* and *Right from the Start: A Pastor's Guide to Premarital Counseling*, both of which were released in 2011.

David and Lisa have published dozens of articles in journals and are frequent contributors to *ParentLife* magazine, published by LifeWay. Their articles on family topics also appear in *Grace & Peace, Holiness Today, Rev, BabyLife*, and other print and online publications. They are frequently quoted by others on topics of single parenting, divorce recovery, and a complex assortment of issues involved in remarriage, blending a family, and growing a healthy stepfamily. Dr. and Mrs. Frisbie enjoy writing and speaking on these topics and do so constantly.

Widely recognized and often quoted about issues of marriage and family life, Dr. and Mrs. Frisbie have traveled extensively to teach, speak, and train counselors, ministers, and leaders, in all fifty United States, nine of Canada's provinces, and more than forty world nations. They have an active interest in serving pastors, missionaries, and other leaders and have been featured presenters at retreats and conferences for pastors and missionaries in North America, Europe, and beyond. They have also served and helped with candidate screening, orientation, debriefing, and member care of field workers and leaders for various NGOs and para-church organizations.

David and Lisa serve the global Church of the Nazarene as co-ordinators of Marriage and Family Ministries. In this role, they are under the leadership and guidance of Larry Morris, director of Adult Ministries for the global church. Their area of responsibility is within Sunday School and Discipleship Ministries (SDMI), which is led by Dr. Woodie Stevens. David and Lisa provide writing, editing, teleconferences, web copy, consulting, speaking, teaching, and training for a wide range of Nazarene settings and situations. They are sought out and consulted by DSs and leaders of various district ministries. They enjoy being speakers and presenters at events including District Sunday School and Discipleship Ministry Conventions and District Ministers and Mates Retreats, among many other venues.

Dr. David Frisbie is an ordained Nazarene minister who has performed more than four hundred weddings to date, both in the United States and overseas. In this capacity, he has led premarriage counseling sessions for couples from many cultures and of many different nationalities. Both David and Lisa travel constantly; both are lifelong learners with a great appreciation for cross-cultural experiences. Whether hiking across the Great Wall of China or sipping an espresso in Sofia, Bulgaria, these two adapt, adjust to, and learn from their local contexts and settings.

Dr. David Frisbie is an adjunct faculty member at Southern Nazarene University, where he teaches courses in marriage and family life for the graduate and professional studies program. In addition, Dr. Frisbie has taught and lectured at colleges, universities, and seminaries worldwide, including teaching classes in premarriage counseling and pastoral counseling.

Both David and Lisa are alumni of MidAmerica Nazarene University; David is a past member of the Board of Trustees for MNU. In addition, David is an alumnus of Nazarene Theological Seminary in Kansas City.

David and Lisa have been named and quoted in *USA Today, The New York Times*, the *St. Paul Pioneer Press*, and numerous other newspapers. They have been interviewed on ABC-TV and CBS-Radio nationally. They have been interviewed on local and national radio broadcasts, including Chuck Bentley's "Money Life" program.

Author appearances and book signing events are held at secular bookstores, including independent retailers, such as Barnes and Noble, in addition to Christian stores such as Mardel, Parable, LifeWay, Berean, Family Christian Stores, and more. Beyond these venues, they do author appearances at church bookstores and at conventions and meetings of global Christian publishing organizations. Both David and Lisa serve as book judges for the Evangelical Christian Publishers Association (ECPA). They have done speaking, personal appearances, and book signings at global events sponsored by the Christian Booksellers Association (CBA) as well as the ECPA and at the annual conference of ICRS—the International Christian Retail Show.

Married since 1978, David and Lisa travel constantly to speak, teach, and counsel. Their life focus is helping marriages and families become healthy; they have a special heart for serving the marriages and families of pastors, missionaries, and others in full-time Christian service. This current book is a labor of love for these two and springs out of more than two decades of serving and helping those who serve in direct, frontline pastoral ministry, as well as those who serve in other contexts, such as cross-cultural ministry and church planting.

Further information is available on the Church of the Nazarene global website under the caption of The Discipleship Place. Among other resources available at this site, Dr. and Mrs. Frisbie have authored a thirty-one-day devotional for married couples that can be accessed at no charge by registering at the site.

Additional information is also available via the business network LinkedIn. You can contact the Frisbies or learn more about their publications and speaking ministry by accessing their business and professional profile in LinkedIn, which is located at the following URL: http:www.LinkedIn.com/in/davidandlisafrisbie.

To reserve a speaking event with these authors, contact: Lisa Douglas—mountainmediagroup@yahoo.com.

For publicity, media events, and book signings by these authors: Laurie Tomlinson—Laurie@keymgc.com.

NOTES

Chapter 2

1. R. C. Angell, *The Family Encounters the Depression*, 2nd ed. (Gloucester, MA: Peter Smith, 1965).

2. R. S. Cavan and K. H. Ranck, *The Family and the Depression: A Study of One Hundred Chicago Families* (Chicago: University of Chicago Press, 1938).

3. Ibid.

4. Ibid.

5. R. Hill, "Generic Features of Families under Stress," *Social Casework* 39 (1958): 139-50.

6. H. I. McCubbin and J. M. Patterson, "Family Adaptation to Crises," in *Family Stress, Coping, and Social Support*, ed. H. I. McCubbin, A. Cauble, and J. M. Patterson (Springfield, IL: Charles C. Thomas, 1982), 26-47.

7. W. R. Burr, "Using Theories in Family Science," in *Research and Theory in Family Science*, eds. R. D. Day, K. R. Gilbert, B. H. Settles, and W. R. Burr (Pacific Grove, CA: Brooks/Cole, 1995), 73-88.

8. M. A. McCubbin and H. I. McCubbin, "Family Stress Theory and Assessment: The T-Double ABCX Model of Family Adjustment and Adaptation," in *Family Assessment Inventories for Research and Practice*, eds. H. I. McCubbin and A. Thompson (Madison: University of Wisconsin, 1987), 3-32.

Chapter 3

1. Eugene H. Peterson, *A Long Obedience in the Same Direction* (Chicago: InterVarsity Press, 1980).

Chapter 8

1. Dr. Woodie Stevens, personal correspondence.

Chapter 9

1. *Journal of Adolescent Health* 35 (Issue 5): 350-59.

The Healthy Pastor seeks to provide insights into the expectations churches and ministers have of the pastor's role. Dennis Bickers addresses some of the common pressure points every minister experiences and provides solutions to those pressures. Ministers will be challenged to create balance in several areas of their lives: their relationship with God, family, the church, themselves, and—for bivocational ministers—their second job.

The Healthy Pastor
Easing the Pressures of Ministry
Dennis Bickers
ISBN 978-0-8341-2553-7

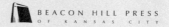

BEACON HILL PRESS
OF KANSAS CITY

www.beaconhillbooks.com
Available online or wherever books are sold.

IT'S TIME FOR A NEW GAME PLAN

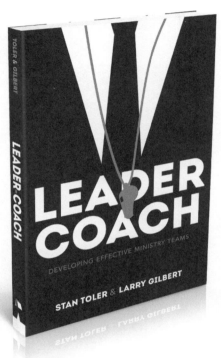

Whether it's in sports or ministry, an effective team is what brings about success. *Leader-Coach* is about the fundamentals of involving the whole congregation in church ministries. With expert advice, practical information, and helpful tips, Stan Toler and Larry Gilbert show how administrators, pastors, and lay leaders can step up their game and lead by bringing out the gifts of those around them.

LEADER-COACH
Stan Toler & Larry Gilbert
ISBN: 978-0-8341-2940-5

AVAILABLE ONLINE AT BEACONHILLBOOKS.COM
ALSO AVAILABLE AS AN EBOOK

BEACON HILL PRESS
OF KANSAS CITY